INTERNATIONAL EDUCATION SERIES

THE EDUCATION OF THE GREEK PEOPLE

AND ITS INFLUENCE ON CIVILIZATION

BY

THOMAS DAVIDSON

AMS PRESS
NEW YORK

Reprinted from the edition of 1894, New York
First AMS EDITION published 1971
Manufactured in the United States of America

International Standard Book Number: 0-404-01944-7

Library of Congress Number: 74-136402

AMS PRESS INC.
NEW YORK, N.Y. 10003

EDITOR'S PREFACE.

THE history of education is best studied when taken in that large sense in which nations are said to be teachers, each people bringing its ethnical contribution to the civilization of the human race. In so far as a nation invents ethical means to overcome the obstacles that it finds to its free development, it offers education to other nations by furnishing an object lesson in solving the problem of life. Such lessons have been furnished by the English nation in achieving what is known as local self-government, inventing devices by which the extreme of individualism is harmonized with the centralized interest of the whole people; by the German nation a quite different lesson, through the perfection of its system of endowing a centralized government with the power of securing in its service those of its citizens possessed of the most powerful wills and wide-seeing intellects; by the French nation another lesson, in training a whole people in the art of tasteful arrangement of all their productions, whether material or spiritual, so as to re-enforce all things useful by the addition of the beautiful.

But there are three nations of ancient time that stand to modern civilization in the relation of teachers

in an eminent sense of the term, and these are Greece,
Rome, and Judea.   The nations of Europe and America of to-day recognize this debt to Judea by setting
apart a learned profession—the highest and most
sacred of all professions, the clergy—to master the
divine message revealed through the highly endowed
spiritual sense of the Hebrews, and in turn to make
the whole people, high and low, acquainted with that
message and able to govern each his own life in accordance with it.   This education in revealed religion
demands and receives one day in seven set apart for
its exclusive purpose, besides its daily recognition in
the presence of secular labor.

Again, our civilization sets apart a learned profession to master the laws by which justice is secured
between man and man.   The protection of life and
property and the punishment of crime, the ordinances
by which individuals combine to form social aggregates
for the prosecution of business, to provide for the welfare of towns, cities, counties, states, and the nation—
all these proceed from a Roman origin, and were, in the
first instance, taught by the Roman prætorian courts
that followed in the wake of Roman armies and made
secure their conquests by establishing Roman jurisprudence in the place of the local laws and customs that
had before prevailed; for the Latin mind had pon-
dered a thousand years on the forms of the will, discovering, one by one, the limitations of individual caprice and arbitrariness necessary to prevent collision
of the individual with the social whole.   The Latin
lesson to the world teaches us how to frame laws and
guide the individual in such ways as to make all his
deeds affirmative of the whole purpose of his commu-

nity and nation, and cause him to inhibit all such deeds as tend toward trespass or any injury of others. This goes to make each person strong through the corporate will of his community and nation. It prevents the collision of each with all—a collision which reduces to zero all reasonable action.

The modern system of education in Europe and America places the study of Latin in all secondary and higher education as a first essential side by side with mathematics in the school studies. This secures for youth from three to seven years' daily occupation with the workings of the Latin mind. The boy or the girl gradually becomes permeated with the motives of that serious-minded people. The special significance of those words that express the ideals of Roman character (and the ideals of all character), words which we have preserved in our translation into English—gravity, soberness, probity, honesty, self-restraint, austerity, considerateness, modesty, patriotism—impresses his mind deeply as a result of long-continued study of Roman literature and history.*

But there is a third people and a third language which we recognize in secondary and higher education. We place the Greek language before the pupil for its influence on his mind in opening it to the vision of science, art, and literature. The Greeks invented all the potent literary forms—epic, lyric, and dramatic. They transformed architecture and sculpture into shapes that reveal spiritual freedom. They

---

* See Rosenkranz, *Philosophy of Education*, vol. i of this series, page 232: "The Latin tongue is crowded with expressions which paint presence of mind, the effort at reflection, a critical attitude of mind, the importance of self-control."

discovered, in fact, the beautiful in its highest forms as the manifestation of freedom or self-determination. Besides the beautiful they also found the true, and explored its forms in science and philosophy. Science and æsthetics treat of the two forms of the intellect, just as jurisprudence treats of the forms of the will. Thus Greece educates all modern nations in the forms of art and literature, while Rome educates them in civil law.

In the beginning Greece is only æsthetic, worshiping beautiful individualities, the gods of Olympus. From the beginning it prizes its athletic games as a sort of worship of the beautiful by realizing gracefulness and physical freedom in the body. Later it fixes in stone and bronze the forms of its athletes as models and sets them up in temples as statues of the gods. Gracefulness is well said to be the expression of spiritual freedom in bodily form. The soul is represented as in complete control of the body, so that every movement and every pose shows the limbs completely obedient to the slightest impulse of the soul. There is other art than Greek; we have Egyptian and Hindu, Chinese, Persian, and Etruscan, but no art that has any success in depicting gracefulness or individual freedom. Even Christian art of Italy, Germany, and France does not attain to supreme gracefulness as does the Greek. For, while Greek art succeeds in representing freedom *in* the body, Romantic art represents freedom from the body, or at least a heart-hunger for such freedom. The martyr saints painted by Fra Angelico and the dead Christs of Volterra, Michel Angelo, and Rubens, all show an expression of relief or divine repose having in view the final liberation from the body. Religion in its essence is a higher form of spiritual activity than art. But Christian art is not so high a form of art as Greek art, because it represents freedom only negatively as separation from the body rather than positively as full incarnation in the body like the Olympian Zeus or the Apollo Belvedere.

Inasmuch as art is the consecration of what is sensuous and physical to the purposes of spiritual freedom, it forever piques the soul to ascend out of the stage of sense - perception into reflection and free thought. To solve the mystery of self-determination in the depths of pure thinking is to grasp the substance of which highest art is only the shadow. Thus the glorious career of Greek philosophy from Thales, through Heraclitus, Pythagoras, and Anaxagoras to its consummation in Socrates, Plato, and Aristotle is the process by which inner reflection attains the same completeness and perfection that art had attained under Pheidias and Praxiteles. Art has, moreover, a link connecting it with philosophy. The dramas of Æschylus and Sophocles grapple with the problems of Greek life, the relation of fate to freedom, the limits of human responsibility and the motives of Divine Providence. Thus art prompts to thought on the questions of ultimate moral import and, in a word, to "theology, or first philosophy," as Aristotle names his treatise on metaphysics.

Prof. Davidson has in this volume sketched in a masterly manner the growth of the Greek civilization through the several stages of the household, the village community, and its culmination in the Athenian city state to its dissolution in the œcumenical or universal empire of Rome. He has discussed the relative value of the ideals of Greek civilization compared with those of the previous civilization out of which it grew, and of the Christian civilization to which it lent one after another many substantial elements. These elements he has characterized as Hellenized Judaism and Zoroastrianism, Neo-Pythagoreanism, and Orientalized Hellenism, all of which entered into conflict with Christianity, but finally gave up to it what they had of permanent value, and disappeared from history. He has shown how the "supernatural sense," or the spiritual sense of the divine as personal God, is the dominating and progressive principle in Christianity, and how it has modified and assimilated the Greek philosophy, from which it has borrowed its logical and scientific forms.

Attention is particularly called to our author's treatment of Diagoge (page 49 and following) as the ideal of Greek life—namely, the occupation of the soul with the contemplation of the beautiful in art and literature, and with the search for the true by the exercise of reflection in science and philosophy—what we call, since the time of Goethe, the aims of culture.

Particular attention is recommended to the discussion of the insights of Socrates in the fifth chapter—namely, his insight into the deeper meaning of the oracle "know thyself," and his insight obtained by the use of the supernatural sense (his "daimon"). He saw that difference of opinion among men, and consequently immorality and civil contention, arises from the fact that men think imperfectly and one-sidedly, and hence do not see the full logical bearing of their own thoughts (see page 108). His famous "dialectic" had for its object the drawing out into consciousness of the complete thought with all its logical implications. In this process the narrow and superficial and immoral views were exposed and refuted and the universally valid truth remained.

This discovery amounts to the demonstration that man possesses "a universal divine element, which is indeed the measure of all things. . . . This was the greatest discovery ever made by any human being, and the one that renders possible moral life, whether individual, social, or political" (page 171). This made possible the assent from opinion to truth; from sophistry to the vision of God.

Finally, the reader is directed to the argument of Chapter VIII, by which the author establishes his doctrine that the failure of the Greeks to furnish an œcumenical or universal religion sufficient for the world empire of the Roman epoch is due to their lack of the supernatural sense, by which the concrete personality of the absolute is apprehended (pages 193–201). The author sums up his conclusions on pages 225, 226 : "Until the supernatural sense can recognize in its object a living God, or being with perfect intelligence, love, and will, supernally correlated, but in no sense identical with the spirits of men, so that His perfections are their goal, and not His being their grave, it will never be able to maintain itself against the abstracting reason or supply the basis of moral life." W. T. HARRIS.

WASHINGTON, D. C., *September, 1894.*

PREFACE.

In my recent book, *Aristotle and the Ancient Educational Ideals*, I endeavored to set forth the facts of Greek education in historical order. The present brief work has an entirely different purpose—which is, to show how the Greek people were gradually educated up to that stage of culture which made them the teachers of the whole world, and what the effect of that teaching has been. Hence education, in its narrow, pedagogic sense, is presented but in the barest outline, while prominence is given to the different stages in the growth of the Greek political, ethical, and religious consciousness, and the effect of this upon Greek history and institutions, as well as upon the after-world.

This work is not intended for scholars or specialists, but for that large body of teachers throughout the country who are trying to do their duty, but are suffering from that want of enthusiasm which necessarily comes from being unable clearly to see the end and purpose of their labors, or to invest any end with sublime import. I have sought to show them that the end of their work is the redemption of humanity, an essential part of that process by which it is being gradually elevated to moral freedom, and to suggest to them the direction in which they ought to turn their chief efforts. If I can make even a few of them feel the consecration that comes from single-minded devotion to a great end, I shall hold that this book has accomplished its purpose.

If any one tell me that my first chapter ought to have been the last in order, I shall not disagree with him. I put it where it is in order that the reader might peruse the rest of them with certain preconceptions in his mind, and that he might clearly know, whenever he met the term "education," what I meant by it. Those who prefer to start with their own conceptions of education may read that lecture last.

I have undertaken a large task in a small compass, and no one can feel more keenly than I do how imperfectly I have accomplished it. Under any circumstances my work must have been a mere sketch; but it is only now that it is finished that I know how much better it might be done by one with resources greater than mine. May the defects of my attempt prove a challenge to such a one to produce a work worthy of the subject!

THOMAS DAVIDSON.

"GLENMORE," KEENE, ESSEX COUNTY, N. Y.,
    May 15, 1893.

CONTENTS.

THE EDUCATION
OF THE GREEK PEOPLE.

CHAPTER I.

INTRODUCTORY.

NATURE AND EDUCATION.

THE term " nature," as applied to living things, is
used in two distinct senses, which in current language
are frequently confounded, to the great detriment of
educational theory and practice. In one sense, it is the
character or type with which a thing starts on its separate career, and which, without any effort on the part
of that thing, but solely with the aid of natural forces,
determines that career. Thus the acorn, the bean, the
chick, the whelp, the cub, possess a definite " nature,"
which in each case manifests itself naturally in the life
of these things. In the other sense, " nature " means
that highest possible reality which a living thing,
through a series of voluntary acts, originating within
or without it, may be made to attain. Thus, through
voluntary acts originating outside of them, many
plants and animals—the rose, the chrysanthemum,
the apple, the orange, the dog, the horse—attain a

2

degree of perfection which would be impossible for them if left to themselves. Similarly, through voluntary acts originating inside of him, man attains a degree of perfection to which his so-called natural instincts could never raise him. If, now, we distinguish these two natures as *original* and *ideal*, we may say that, in the world known to us, man is the only being able to originate the acts whereby he is raised from his original to his ideal nature. The sum or system of these acts is what we call education, and this is perhaps the best definition of that term, in its widest sense, that can be given. When man employs these acts to raise creatures other than himself, we call the result culture, training, breeding, etc.

We often hear it said that the aim of education is to develop the "nature" of the child, that his "nature" must not be crossed, that whatever he is called upon to do must be "natural," and so on. If the distinction above made is correct, it is obvious that, in employing such phrases, we must keep it clearly before our minds, unless we are to be champions of confusion. If we mean that the purpose of education is to develop the child's nature, in the first sense of that term, we mean something that is altogether false and perverse. It is only when we use "nature" in the second sense that such phrases express truth. The aim of education is to develop man's ideal nature, which may be, and very often is, so different from his original nature that, in order to make way for the former, the latter may have to be crossed, defied, and even to a large extent suppressed. Tried by the standard of the original nature, the ideal nature is frequently and largely unnatural. When the Apostle Paul (1 Cor. ii, 14) says, "The natural man receiveth not the things of the Spirit of God," he is only expressing this truth in the language of religion; and the whole doctrine of Original Sin is founded upon the same. The fact is, nothing could be more prejudicial to the best interests of education than any attempt to evoke indiscriminately the tendencies of the child's original nature. Hence, all the popular talk about developing the child's "spontaneity" is little more than sentimental cant, likely enough to do incalculable mischief.

Education, then, in so far as it depends upon conscious exertion, is that process by which a human being is enabled to transcend his original nature and attain his ideal nature, or be the most desirable thing that he can be. This end attained is his Good. If this be true, the first question that presents itself to the educator is: Wherein does man's ideal nature, or good, consist? and the second: How does this stand related to his original nature? The second presents no difficulty when the first is answered; but the first is so far from easy that many and widely divergent answers have been given to it. The Buddha, for example, makes man's good consist in the complete suppression of selfhood; Plato, in the vision of eternal ideas, those everlasting and perfect models of which the things of sense are but transient and imperfect copies; Aristotle, in the exercise of man's highest or characteristic faculty, viz., his reason; Zeno, in a life according to nature—a life attainable only through the supremacy of reason, which alone cognizes the order of nature; Epicurus, in the enjoyment of calm, abiding pleasure; Jesus, in absolute submission to the will of God; Dante and the mediæval saints, in the vision

or enjoyment of God (*Deo frui*); Goethe, Comte, and
most modern humanitarians, in devotion to the well-
being, variously defined, of humanity; many English,
French, and Italian thinkers of last century and this,
in pleasure, variously conceived; Kant, in a good will;
Hegel, in conscious freedom; Von Hartmann, in submission to suffering, for the sake of relieving God from
misery, and enabling him to reach unconsciousness
and annihilation; and so on. Widely different as these
views seem to be, we shall find, on examining them,
that they have an important tenet in common. They
all hold that man's ideal nature can be realized only
in a system of relations including himself and his
environment—that is, his not-self. They differ only in
the manner in which they conceive the self and the
not-self, their nature and possibilities. When, for
example, Epicurus tells men to look for their highest
condition in such a relation to their inner and outer
world as shall secure them abiding pleasure, and when
Jesus tells them to look for it in a relation of absolute
conformity to the will of God, the only difference in
the two counsels lies in the fact that the one conceives
the world as essentially sensuous, the other as essentially moral and divine. Both alike bid men look for
their highest condition in a harmonious relation to the
world or universe, as they respectively conceive it—the
one counseling selfish prudence, the highest possible
virtue in a sensuous world; the other, morality and
self-devotion, which imply a divine world.

Inasmuch, then, as the divergent answers given to
the question, Wherein consists man's ideal nature?
are due to different conceptions of the universe and
man's place in it, we shall not obtain any satisfactory

answer to it until we reach the true conception of the nature of the universe—until, at least, we make up our minds whether it is, in its essence, material and sensuous, or spiritual and moral. In trying to decide this question, we shall appeal in vain to the conflicting views of philosophers and would-be philosophers. Rather must we turn to the common consciousness of mankind, as revealed in its moral estimates and practice. And here, if we listen without prejudice, we shall meet with no uncertain answer. Whatever thinkers of the Epicurean school may say in favor of their view, men, in proportion as they advance in civilization, do more and more despise him who seeks his chief good in pleasure, and more and more honor him who, indifferent to pleasure, seeks and finds his satisfaction in moral action. And the facts of human life and history confirm this verdict of the common consciousness. Individuals or nations devoted to pleasure, as their supreme good, soon sink into degradation or slavery, while those devoted to rational ends prosper, and hold their own, often against fearful odds.

Trusting to the double testimony of the common consciousness and of history, we may rationally conclude that, in its deepest essence, the world is moral and spiritual, and that the relations whose realization constitutes man's "ideal nature," or good, are moral relations. In saying, then, that education is the process by which human beings are raised from their original nature to their ideal nature, we mean that it is what raises them from a sensuous life, governed by instinct, to a moral life, governed by reason. It is now easy enough to answer our second question, and

to determine the relation in which man's ideal nature
stands to his original nature. It is a relation of master
to servant. It is the part of the ideal nature to command; of the original nature, to obey. This must not
be understood to mean that the original nature is to
be regarded as base and sinful, and to be starved or
haughtily suppressed, as is often assumed by men of
the ascetic type. On the contrary, since life in its
highest conceivable form is but passion guided by
reason, and reason has no other function than to
guide passion, the richness of the higher and commanding nature will be exactly proportioned to the
number, complexity, and robustness of the passions
that have to be regulated. It is only the dispropor-
tionate robustness of particular passions that has to
be suppressed.

In saying that man's ideal nature is his moral
nature, we have by no means made clear what is implied by the latter term. And there are few terms
connected with education which stand more in need
of clear definition. It is not unusual to hear the
moral nature of man spoken of as if it were something independent of the rest of his being, something
that could be cultivated by itself, apart from his intelligence and his sensuous nature. Nor is it difficult
to see why this mistake has been made. People are
continually tempted to confound actions which con-
form to a recognized standard, or which contribute to
social well-being, with moral actions. Now, it is certainly true that actions of the former kind are prefer-
able to lawless or anarchic actions, and also that their
performance may, to a large extent, be secured by a
one-sided training through habit, or even by appeal to

a single passion—namely, fear. Not to speak of sav-
ages and barbarians, who, through sheer force of tribal
custom, habitually perform such actions, and are
therefore held, to a certain degree justly, to possess
many virtues, we see that even dogs, cats, and other
brute creatures can be trained by habit, or by pleasure
and pain, to perform them. But although in the case
of men such training forms an excellent preparation
for moral life, and may therefore fairly be considered
a part of education, it does not in itself insure such
life, since moral life can not be brought about by any
such process. Moral life is life consciously conducted
in conformity with the laws by which man can live as
a rational being, and increase the plenitude of that
being, and such life depends upon the cultivation of
all his powers, mental and bodily.

A very little consideration will convince us that this
is true : Man's spiritual faculties * naturally range
themselves in three classes—(1) rational, (2) emotional
or affectional, (3) volitional or active. His bodily powers, for our present purpose, may be regarded as all
belonging to one class, though they naturally enough
fall into two—the receptive and the motor. Each of
these faculties faces, so to speak, two ways—toward
the world of nature and toward the world of spirit.
Reason, for example, obtains through the bodily senses
the data with which it spontaneously constructs the
natural world ; through the spiritual sense,† those

---

* On the right to use this term, see Martineau, *Types of
Ethical Theory*, vol. ii, pp. 11 *sqq.*

† This from the days of Jerome onward was called by the
Church thinkers *synderesis* (συντήρησις) ; in the Middle Age,
sometimes the apex of the mind (*apex mentis*). See an excellent

through which it voluntarily constructs the spiritual world.* And what reason constructs, love aspires to, and will seeks to realize in concrete form. There is a natural love and there is a spiritual love,† a natural will and a spiritual will.‡ Between these two worlds— that of nature and that of spirit—man's lot is cast. They furnish the conditions under which he is called upon to live, and his life consists in a more or less perfect adaptation to them. Much is said at the present day of the "survival of the fittest." The fittest are those who stand in the most complete relation to the two worlds. Now, it is clear enough that a man can not live in accordance with the conditions of rational life without knowing them, and that he can not know them unless his intelligence is cultivated. As civilization advances, these conditions become more and more complicated, and therefore demand for their comprehension an ever-increasing cultivation of the intelligence. The cultivation that sufficed to enable a man to live rationally in the time of Homer, or Plato, or Cæsar, or Alfred, or even of Washington, is altogether insufficient for the man of the present day, and there can be no greater or more fatal mistake in education than to ignore this fact. Every age demands an education of the intelligence suited to its own conditions.

---

essay on the *Culture of the Spiritual Sense*, in Brother Azarias's *Phases of Thought and Criticism*, pp. 72–88.

* In making this distinction between the natural and spiritual worlds, I am not championing any form of ultimate dualism. Indeed, the whole question of dualism and monism seems to me little less than stupid, a mere contest about words.

† See Dante, Purg., xvii, 91 *sqq.*

‡ Ibid., xxi, 61 *sqq.*

But it is not enough for a man to understand the conditions of rational life in his own time; he must likewise love these conditions, and hate whatever leads to life of an opposite kind. This is only another way of saying that he must love the good and hate the evil; for the good is simply what conduces to rational or moral life, and the evil merely what leads away from it. But he can not do this unless his affectional nature is carefully trained, so that he loves each person and thing with whom or which he has to deal in proportion to his or its value for moral ends. It is perfectly obvious, as soon as it is pointed out, that all immoral life is due to a false distribution of affection, which again is often, though by no means always, due to a want of intellectual cultivation. He that attributes to anything a value greater or less than it really possesses in the order of things has already placed himself in a false relation to it, and will certainly, when he comes to act with reference to it, act immorally. But, again, it is not enough for a man to understand correctly and love duly the conditions of moral life in his own time; he must, still further, be willing and able to fulfill these conditions. And he certainly can not do this unless his will is trained to perfect freedom, so that it responds, with the utmost readiness, to the suggestions of his discriminating intelligence and the movements of his chastened affections. But even this is not enough; or rather, perhaps, we ought to say that not one of these spiritual conditions can be realized unless the powers of the body are in full health and strength. When the blood is sluggish, the nerves weak, or the digestion impaired, then the intellect is clouded, the affections are morbid, the will is enfeebled. " The whole head is sick and the whole heart faint."

Moral life, therefore—man's ideal nature—demands for its realization the education of all his powers, bodily and mental. Having established this general but important conclusion, we must next descend to particulars and inquire what sort of education each of the faculties must receive, in order that it may contribute its due share to the desired result; in a word, how the body, the intellect, the affections, and the will must be trained. Now, inasmuch as they must obviously be trained with due regard to their natural hierarchy and order of development, we must begin our inquiry by asking, What is the natural hierarchy of the human powers? In what order do they naturally develop? And these questions are so far from being easy to answer that widely different replies, both theoretical and practical, have been given to them at different periods and by different educators. Some have thought that education ought to begin with the body; others, with the intellect, or at least some faculty of it; others, with the will; and others, with the affections; and not a few have thought that certain faculties might without danger be neglected altogether, or left to take care of themselves. In a large part of mediæval Europe, and even till recently among ourselves, bodily education was neglected or even contemned, while at the present day the affections and the will are almost everywhere suffering from a similar neglect.

In trying to reach a correct conclusion in this matter, we must beware of assuming that the natural hierarchy of the powers necessarily coincides with their order of development. This is, indeed, a matter for

careful consideration, in which the first step is to discover the order in which the powers naturally develop.
And this is easy enough; for it is obvious that the
bodily powers or functions—digestion, secretion, etc.—
develop first; then that portion of the intellectual faculties which accomplishes sense perception, and simultaneously with these the natural instincts or prefer-
ences; and lastly, if ever, the reflective faculties of the
intellect and their correlate, the will.* It is clear,
also, that this order of development coincides with the
natural hierarchy of the human powers. Reverting
now to our previous distinction between the original
and the ideal nature of man, we can readily see that
education, in aiming to realize the latter, seeks to do
so by substituting for the natural order of development
an order which may fairly enough be called supernatural, if by that we mean belonging to a higher order in
nature; for, indeed, the whole aim of education is to
develop intellectual reflection and will from the earliest
possible moment in life, and to apply them from the
very first to the regulation of the lower faculties. In
saying this, we are, of course, only saying, in other
words, that the aim of education is to make men intelligent and moral beings, instead of beings living by
sense and instinct, or wilfulness.

What has just been said enables us to deal intelligently with the often-repeated pedagogical maxim,
that education must seek to unfold the powers of the
child in accordance with their natural order of develop-

---

* We must not, of course, confound will with wilfulness.
The latter is the very opposite of will, being mere unregulated
instinct.

ment. Before we can accept such a maxim we must understand in what sense the word "natural" is used, whether it refers to man's original, or to his ideal, nature. Indeed, we can accept it only if it is used with reference to the latter. It is not true that education should seek to call forth the powers of the child according to their order of development in his original nature; that is, to evoke sense perception and instinct before reflection and will. On the contrary, it should seek to introduce reflection into every act of perception, and will into every movement of instinct, from the earliest possible moment. It is to a neglect of this important distinction that are due the stress which has of recent years been laid upon mere object-teaching as a means of "educating the senses," and the well-meant, but fatal, attempts of kindly parents to educate their children by leaving them to the guidance of their own "spontaneity."

In any order of development of the human powers, those of the body, in so far as they are purely instinctive, must obviously precede all others. Sensation, movement, nutrition are the very conditions of life, the vital foundation upon which all higher life is built up. So long as they exist alone (and they do so exist for some time), the human creature is incapable of conscious education, though by no means insensible to such treatment as may make this education easier, when higher faculties come into play. It is only when the powers of sense perception begin to be roused that conscious education can be undertaken, because it is only then that there is any intelligent consciousness to work upon. It is one of the great triumphs of modern psychology to have shown that what is termed sense perception is not a series of impressions made by external things upon a blank, passive tablet, but that, in so far as it is perception, and not merely sense, it is the work of the ordering or creating understanding. It follows directly from this that, to a very large extent, every human being creates his own world; and since his moral life greatly depends upon the world he creates and has to live in, it plainly becomes the chief function of education to aid him in creating such a world as may enable him to live a life of the noblest kind. If it be asked how education can exert an influence upon the creation of individual worlds, the answer is that, since every man's world is composed of those elements to which his attention is chiefly directed, and by those processes which are most habitual, and therefore most easy, to him, education may greatly influence the creative process for good by directing the child's attention from the first to the nobler impressions, and habituating him to those processes of mind which are best calculated to arrange these into an orderly, or perhaps we may say at once a rational, world. If the "original nature" of the child be permitted, without regulation or control, to create his world for him, the result will, in the main, be a world of strong impressions, arranged by the caprice of instinctive passion, counterbalanced only, in the best cases, by the dull routine of tribal customs. Such, indeed, we find to be the worlds of the members of those savage tribes in which "original nature" is allowed to have free play. To obviate the creation of such worlds, it is essential that the higher faculties of the child—his intelligence and his will—be *artificially* called into play from the earliest possible moment, and made to control his original nature, for the sake of his ideal nature. This is just what education means. The ideal order of development, therefore, among the human faculties differs from the original one in this: that whereas, in the latter the faculties of perception and instinct are developed before those of intellect and will, in the former they are all developed simultaneously, and in such a way that the higher control the lower.

It will, of course, be said, and justly, that the process of evoking the intellect and will of the child in such a way that they shall control his impressions and instincts is a very slow and, in many cases, a very difficult one; but it by no means follows that, until such time as the process is complete, his impressions and instincts are to be left to take care of themselves. It is just here that the intellect and will of parents come in as substitutes and fulfill their most important function; for, indeed, there is no time at which the influence of parents is so effectual and decisive as when it is enabling the child, whose intelligence and will are yet embryonic, to lay a worthy foundation for his future world, by directing his attention to the things that are fair and good, and training his intellect to note the relations of these things. And this is just what the *Kindergarten*, when properly conducted, undertakes to do.

We are now, I trust, in a position to sketch, in its broad outlines, the process by which the human being is lifted out of his original nature and advanced to his ideal nature—that is, to trace the course of a true education.

When the human creature comes into the world, and for some time after, it is hardly more than an

animal, with animal needs; and as such it has to be
treated. Indeed, it is the most helpless of all young
animals, and requires the greatest amount of attention. This attention, the first step in education,
should be directed to promoting its bodily health and
warding off such influences as would interfere with its
normal growth. Warmth, sleep, and good digestion are
the three principal things of which it stands in need
at this period, and it needs them all the more, if it has
come into the world weighted, as so many children are,
with hereditary weakness. After a few months it begins to show signs of intelligence. It is now proceeding
to build up its own world by means of selective attention, and this attention may be artificially directed and
prolonged, so that a rational world shall result. At this
stage the aims of the educator ought to be (1) to direct
the child's attention to things on which it is well that
attention should rest, and which yield impressions fitted
to give a healthy fundamental tone and temper to the
whole character, and (2) to sustain that attention as
long as possible. Thus the child's earliest impressions
—those round which all succeeding ones cluster, and by
which they are necessarily colored—will be such as shall
not require subsequent removal or correction, and his
will will receive a most valuable exercise, the only one
of which at that stage it is capable. It ought, indeed,
never be forgotten that most of the difficulties with
which education in its later stages has to contend are
due to two causes : (1) the presence in the child's mind
of undesirable and chaotic impressions, which have to
be removed and corrected before an orderly world can
be built up in it; (2) the absence of the power of continued attention, or, which is the same thing, the ab-

sence of power of will. The original nature of the child, in its pure fickleness and caprice, demands a continual change of impressions, and the best way to replace this caprice by will is to cultivate prolonged attention to single impressions or groups of impressions. Nor must the teacher ever forget, what is an axiom in all education, that such attention is best secured by action. The objects, therefore, to which the child's attention is directed should be such as he can do something about, not such as he can merely look at or listen to. Moreover, in doing something about things, he is at once exercising his active faculties and finding opportunities for moral choice. The utmost care, therefore, ought to be taken in selecting playthings and games for him. These ought not to be numerous. Two playthings are better than twenty; and one game with a purpose is better than fifty without. It is not too much to say that prolonged attention, accompanied with action, being the first exercise of will on the part of the child, is the prime condition of all intellectual and moral progress.

In selecting objects upon which to direct the young child's wakening attention, the wise parent or teacher will bear in mind that the intellect has two closely allied functions—(1) to recognize distinctions and relations of fact, (2) to recognize distinctions and relations of worth. Bearing in mind, further, that the latter, being essentially the moral faculty, is the more important of the two, he will give preference to such objects and occupations as are calculated to fix the child's attention not only upon relations of fact, but also, and still more, upon relations of worth. In a word, he will aim at evoking the child's affections, which are his worth-giving faculties, in a manner proportioned to the moral distinctions between things, and he will do this as the best means of directing his attention to distinctions of fact. By thus enlisting the affections of the child in the interest of education, he at once obtains two important advantages: (1) he comes into possession of the key to his will, and so renders him, in the main, his own instructor and guide; and (2) he makes his entire life rest on a moral foundation. Notwithstanding the extreme importance of this method, it has in the past received but little attention, and even at the present day it is astonishing to see how little care is taken by parents and teachers to moralize, from the first, the child's affections, and to make them the prime agents in education.

In his *Education of Cyrus*, Xenophon tells us that, whereas Greek boys went to school to learn letters, Persian boys went to learn justice. Xenophon, indeed, is merely romancing in this case; but he does suggest, nevertheless, an important pedagogical truth, viz., that during the early years of a child's life—say from the end of his second to that of his seventh year—the chief aim of education ought to be to call out and guide his affections in accordance with the true worth of things, and to make him recognize in his actions the distinctions thus established; and this will have to be done mainly by precept, persuasion, and example, not by any appeal to reason. While this process is going on, attention will have to be directed to physical culture, with a view to health, grace, and ease of movement. Sluggishness and restlessness will alike be avoided, and no attempt will be made to cultivate the athletic habit.

3

In the period following the completion of the child's seventh year (the epoch will differ somewhat for different children), education will take a new direction. Instruction will take the place of training. The educator will now endeavor to acquaint the child with the rational grounds for those distinctions and corresponding actions with which his previous training has made him familiar, and to prepare the way for action of a wider scope based upon rational knowledge. But the rational grounds for moral distinctions are neither more nor less than the relations, or, which is the same thing, the laws of the universe. It is therefore into these that the child must now be gradually initiated. Now, the laws of the universe are divided into physical and metaphysical (or spiritual), and this involves a similar division of studies.

But before any study whatsoever can be successfully carried forward, the child must be taught to use the instruments of study, which may be said to be three: (1) language, (2) number, and (3) manual facility. Of course, he will already, especially if he has attended a Kindergarten, be, to some extent, familiar with all these. He will be able to talk, to perform the simple arithmetical processes, and perhaps to mold clay, braid straw, and do similar things. Now he must learn to read and write, to perform the more difficult arithmetical operations, to draw, and to practice one or more of the material arts.* It is due to a stupid preju-

---

* In distinguishing the arts into material and spiritual, instead of into "useful" and "liberal" or "fine," I know that I am departing from long-established usage; but surely it is high time that we were setting aside terms implying a view of life which it is the aim of our civilization and our education to render obso-

dice, inherited from antiquity, against these arts that their great educational value has not been seen. This value is threefold : they impart (1) mechanical skill; (2) a habit of carefulness and thoughtfulness, closely akin to conscientiousness; and (3) a knowledge of the forms of things and a sense of the adaptation of means to ends, such as could hardly be obtained in any other way. It is needless to say that drawing and manual training, if properly taught, will form an excellent introduction to the study of art and nature.

As soon as young people have attained a mastery of these instruments of study, they will apply them to the world without and within them, to obtain a knowledge of its laws, physical and metaphysical. In order to learn the laws of their physical constitution, they will direct their attention to the natural sciences, in the order of their complexity, beginning with those which deal with mere mechanical forces, and gradually advancing toward those which include instinct and life; in order to learn those of their spiritual being, they will study grammar, logic,* æsthetics, ethics, and religion. From the physical sciences they will learn

---

lete, as casting an unmerited and unbrothering slur upon the useful and those engaged in the production of it, and as suggesting that the useful is illiberal and coarse, and the liberal and fine useless. All art is useful, all art is liberal, all art is fine, else it has no business to be at all.

* The characteristic and fatal neglect of logic in modern school education can hardly be excused on the ground of its difficulty. In reality it is not more difficult than grammar, along with which and with rhetoric it formed the *Trivium* of the Middle Ages. Even Luther recommends that "as soon as boys are sufficiently grounded in grammar, the hour previously devoted to it shall be used for logic and rhetoric."

the laws of sensation—that is, of those impulses which rouse the action of reflective thought, and constitute, so to speak, its material; from grammar, the nature and use of the means whereby thought expresses itself in speech; from logic, the laws of thought itself; from æsthetics, the laws determining the relative worth of things or beings for emotion; from ethics, the laws governing the active relations of finite beings; and from religion, the laws governing the whole of the relations of finite rational beings to the Infinite Being.

After what has been already said, it will hardly be necessary to insist that every branch of study ought to be at once a science and an art, calling into play not only the passive and receptive faculties, but also the active and creative ones. Even in study it is more blessed to give than to receive. "Mere knowledge," in which action and creation bear no part, has always been justly despised. It may, however, be necessary to say a few words regarding the content of some of the above-named branches of study, especially of the spiritual ones. Under grammar I mean to include all linguistic study—in a word, what is often abusively termed philology; under logic, not only formal logic, so called, and dialectic, but also ideology, inductive logic, and the methodology of the sciences; under æsthetics, the theory and, to some extent, the practice of the spiritual arts—literary, musical, graphic, and plastic; under ethics, not only morals, politics, and economics, but also pedagogics, social science, and the history of civilization, or, as it might fairly be called, of the ethical world; and lastly, under religion, the laws of the spiritual sense and of the world of which it supplies the material. The theoretical side of religion is theology; the practical, the divine life.

It will be observed that in the above enumeration one science, which at the present day receives much attention, has been omitted—viz., psychology. I have done this because, in my opinion, psychology is not a single science, but a mere name for a group of sciences, all of which are included in the above list—zoölogy, biology, physiology, ideology, logic, ethics, etc.

The cycle of studies, thus completed and closed by theology, constitutes an ordered whole, corresponding to the ordered whole of the universe, as far as it is known at any given moment, and is calculated to make him who pursues it a complete human being, harmonious inwardly and outwardly, being related by all his powers, physical and spiritual, to the universe in which he lives and moves and has his being. In a word, it marks the stages in the process by which man ascends from his original to his ideal nature. In saying this, however, we must not fail to realize that the cycle of the sciences is never, in reality, completed or closed, that everywhere there are large gaps in it. The widest and most regrettable of these is the gap between the spiritual and the natural sciences. Here so great a gulf is fixed that, however firmly we may believe that the facts of spirit come under the laws of nature, or those of nature under those of spirit, we are utterly unable to see how this is possible.

In the above rapid sketch of the educative process, little has been said about physical training; nothing about the distinction between education and erudition; and no attempt has been made to map out an accurate plan of study having regard to the age of pupils and the grade of institutions. We must now briefly consider these points.

With regard to physical training, the fundamental principle to be laid down is, that its aim is not to produce athletes, mountebanks, or exquisites, but to render the body the ready, obedient, supple, and effective minister of the soul, at the same time imparting to it such dignity and grace as shall make the presence of its owner at once impressive and agreeable. With a view to this end, four things—food, sleep, warmth, and exercise—require to be regulated in accordance with the different grades of physical development. But a good physical trainer will take into account, not only the age of his pupils, but also their temperaments, characters, and the entire round of their daily activity, and will so harmonize physical training with intellectual labor that the two shall aid, instead of impending, each other. At all periods of life he will insist upon a robust cleanliness, having no affinity with that feverish fastidiousness which often forgets the claims of humanity in those of neatness. Seeing that physical training is apt to develop a spirit of emulation, which not unfrequently degenerates into vanity, arrogance, and bullying, he will use every effort to suppress this spirit and to make his pupils feel that their training is meant to enable them, not to triumph by bodily strength over their fellows, but to raise their fellows to all that is great and worthy. He will therefore continually remind them and—himself ! that the training of nerves and of temper, which depends upon nerves, is far more important than the development of muscle. In barbarous days, before brutality and violence were checked by law, muscle was a possession of prime importance; at present, it can be little more than a minister to vanity, that vice which has survived most other manifestations of barbarism.

Between education and erudition a clear line needs to be drawn. Education, as we have seen, is the process by which a human being is lifted out of his original into his ideal nature, and is something which every human being ought to claim and strive after. Erudition, on the other hand, is that special learning which renders its possessor an authority, and enables him to become an original investigator, in any special department of science. It is a specialty and generally a preparation for a particular profession. A man of education at the present day requires, for example, to know French and German sufficiently well to be able to read with ease books written in them; but he need not know the entire history and philology of these languages, as Littré knew French, and the Grimms German. So every educated man must know history and biology; but he is not bound to be a Mommsen or a Darwin. It is the failure to draw this necessary distinction between education and erudition that is misleading our universities into the error of allowing students to "elect" specialties before they have completed the cycle of education, the result of which is that we have few men of thorough education or of broad and comprehensive views. If this evil is ever to be remedied, our universities will be obliged either to abandon this practice, or else to give up all attempt to impart education, and devote themselves solely to erudition, leaving the other to academies, gymnasia, or the like.

And this leads us to consider the order in which

the various studies constituting a complete education
ought to be pursued. We can touch the subject only
lightly, and shall, for convenience' sake, divide the
time of education by years and institutions, thus:

First period, seven years, family and Kindergarten.
Second "   three   "   primary school.
Third   "   four   "   grammar school.
Fourth "   four   "   high school, academy, or gymnasium.
Fifth   "   four   "   university, with fixed curriculum.

1. The first period will be devoted mainly to the
development of the physical and moral faculties of the
child and of its power of fixed attention. Its physical
faculties will be fostered by much sleep, simple food
suited to its years, and gentle activity taking the form
of play; its moral faculties, by the direction of its affections upon worthy things and by habituation to
right actions; and its power of attention, by stories
and actions that terminate in a way that can not fail
to interest. Nothing so much interests a child as a
result obtained by a process, especially a process gone
through by itself. The education of this period will
be conducted almost entirely by the reason of the
parent or teacher, not by that of the child, whose chief
virtues will now be reverence and obedience. These
are the foundations of all the virtues.

2. The second period will be occupied chiefly with
learning the use of the instruments of study—reading,
writing, drawing, arithmetic, and manual facility. If
entire carefulness, thoroughness, and conscientiousness
be insisted on in the acquisition of these, hardly any
other special training will be required to keep the
moral faculties in a healthy condition. A child who
does honest work, and sees the result of it, can hardly

fail at once to obtain an oracle of approval from his own conscience, and to see the rationality of well-doing. In this way he gradually comes to be his own moral director, and so to be a free being.

3. The task of the third period will be to make the growing boy and girl familiar with their own mental processes—intellectual, æsthetic, and moral—and to give them general notions of the world in which they live. Grammar, logic, the first principles of æsthetics and ethics; astronomy (involving geometry and mechanics), physical and political geography, and the outlines of history, enlivened by biographies of great men, will form the chief subjects of study. In connection with the first four subjects a good deal of reading in prose and poetry will be done, and many literary gems committed to memory. The years from ten to fourteen being those in which the memory is most retentive, the opportunity ought to be seized for storing it with the best and best-expressed thought of all the ages. It is not necessary that the whole of it should be at once understood; lodged in the memory, it may safely be left to germinate and grow, as the experience of life gives it meaning, by furnishing concrete illustrations of it. Now also is the time for committing to memory the paradigms of those languages an acquaintance with which forms an essential means to a complete education—Greek, Latin, German, etc. Physical training will now take the form of regular gymnastics (*Turnen*), supplemented by swimming, riding, vigorous games, dancing, and some such manual labor as wood-chopping, carpentering, gardening, etc. This may seem a large programme for such tender years; but experience will show that it may be successfully

carried out, if every waking hour is filled, as it ought to be, with aimful, rational work. Nothing is more fatal at this age than aimless action and listless lounging. They are the parents of mischief and waywardness.

4. The fourth or high-school period is, for many reasons, the most difficult to deal with. It is the period in which the transition is made from boyhood and girlhood to manhood and womanhood, when new feelings and interests are awakened and come with a kind of surprise, when both youth and maiden find themselves in a new world, for which their previous training and habits have hardly prepared them, and in which, therefore, they are most liable to go astray, unless proper precaution be taken. The leading characteristic of all the studies of this period should be vigor, calling for a strong exercise of will, and a good deal of energetic emotion. Geology, chemistry, botany, and zoölogy, involving considerable outdoor life, are now in order ; so is history—political, social, and economic—with its heart-stirring heroisms and pathos and its noble examples of manliness and womanliness, of tenderness and generosity. Now is the time to read the great epics, dramas, and orations of the world, and to commit the best parts of them to memory ; now the time to form an acquaintance with the great works of sculpture and painting ; now the time to give the imagination free scope by reading and rereading the works of Sir Walter Scott ; now the time for such physical exercises and games as demand courage, endurance, and patience, and at the same time give ample opportunity for exercising the sense of justice.

5. The chief aim of the studies of the fifth period will be to round off into an harmonious and consistent view of the world all that has gone before, and so prepare the young man and woman to enter upon life as upon a rational task, to be undertaken for rational ends. The leading characteristic of the occupations of this period will be comprehensiveness, calling for quiet, steady reflection and calm, dignified action. Biology, the higher problems of ethics, sociology and politics, theology and the history of religion, psychology, epistemology, and the various systems of speculative philosophy will now be studied. The chief works on evolution, the sacred books of the great religions, the masterpieces of Plato, Aristotle, the great Schoolmen, Descartes, Spinoza, Locke, Hume, Leibnitz, Reid, Kant, Hegel, and Rosmini; the writings of the great poet philosophers—the *Oresteia*, the *De Rerum Natura*, the *Divine Comedy*, *Faust*, *In Memoriam* —will be read and carefully discussed. Now will be cultivated the power of orderly, forcible, and perspicuous writing and speaking, and that modesty combined with confidence which makes both effective. Physical exercise will now consist mainly of walking, riding, swimming, rowing, and light gymnastics. Violent exercise will gradually be discarded, and quiet endurance, more than spasmodic strength, be cultivated. In the sphere of morals and religion every means will be used to make the young man and young woman feel, see, and by action prove, that the world is God's home, mankind His family, and He the infinite, loving Father. Thus will arise that persistent attitude of love and worship which alone confers consecration and blessedness on life, which alone gives

man the right to say that he is educated, that he has conquered his original nature, and risen to his ideal nature.   A divine world will now have been created in the individual soul, and therein life will be truly aimful and blessed, because it is the life of God.

CHAPTER II.

THE outline of a program of education given in the last chapter was meant to furnish us with a standard whereby to estimate the educational system of the Greeks. Therein we sought to show that the aim of education is to lift the human being out of his "original nature" into his "ideal nature," which consists of intelligence, affection, and will, harmoniously working together for their own perfection; and we concluded that the best education is that which best accomplishes this object.

Before proceeding further, we may do well to dwell for a moment longer on this fundamental point. Man, as a rational being, is his own end. The aim of his life is the realization or manifestation of himself, and to this aim all things, all art, all science, nay, the world itself, are subservient. This self-manifestation forms a triunity of intelligence, affection, will; and it is on the scale of this triunity that all human worth, whether in individuals, nations, or epochs, is measured. If we wish to know where an individual stands in the scale of worth ($\dot{a}\rho\epsilon\tau\dot{\eta}$), we have only to find out how much intelligence, how much love, sympathy, or affection, how much will he possesses, and how harmoniously these are blended. And the same thing is true of nations and epochs. God himself can mean to us nothing more, and nothing less, than the complete and harmonious realization of intelligence, love, and will; for these are the constituent elements of true being, of which He is the plenitude.

These considerations suggest a curious and somewhat paradoxical result, viz., that a man's sole and only possible duty in this world is to realize himself; in other words, to manifest in himself the divine image, the plenitude of being. At the first glance, this seems to mean that a man's sole concern is with himself and his own " culture," and that he can well afford to neglect the rest of the world, or to use it merely as means. But a moment's reflection will show that the truth is far otherwise. For how can a man manifest intelligence except by knowing the world, man, and God ; or love, except by loving these ; or will, except by serving these ? It follows that the individual can realize himself only by knowing, loving, and serving the world, man, and God. Moreover, since the end of life is the realization of the divine plenitude, it is this that sets the standard of duty, this that furnishes its sanction. In a word, all duty is primarily and directly duty to God. Man's duty to man is but secondary and indirect. It is this fact that imparts to duty its dignity, lifting it out of the spasmodic currents of sentiment and the beggarly arithmetic of prudence, and making it the expression of the divine will which neither hastes nor rests.

The fact that man can attain his end only through knowing, loving, and serving God and his fellows forms the reason why he creates institutions—why he is, as Aristotle said, "a political animal." Institutions are means whereby men are enabled to know, love, and serve God and their fellows better, and are valuable just in proportion as they accomplish this. Here, then, we have a standard for measuring the worth of institutions.

With these standards for moral worth, for duty, and for institutions in our minds, we may perhaps approach Greek education with some hope of forming a true estimate of it. But, before we can do this, we must be able to form a clear conception of what that education was, in what condition it found its subjects, and what it undertook to do for them. This will compel us to consider Greek Life and its Ideals, which, accordingly, will form the subject of this chapter.

During the period in which the Greeks had anything that could fairly be called an educational system, as distinguished from the training afforded by experience, their life centered in, and revolved round, a single institution, which, for want of a better term, we may call the city-state (πόλις). This, the highest political achievement of Greek genius, was the crown of a long process, the various epochs in which were marked by institutions of lower grade. These the city-state absorbed, modified, and subordinated, so that they became its organs. In order, then, to understand Greek life and its ideals, we must consider this institution and these organs.

Aristotle, in the opening chapter of his *Politics*, tells us that the steps in political evolution are marked by (1) the household (οἶκος, οἰκία, γένος), (2) the village community or township (κώμη, δῆμος), and (3) the city-state (πόλις) ; and he goes on to say that the first aims

at securing the natural and daily necessities of life;
the second, at providing for the more permanent material goods; the third, at making possible independence or freedom and a virtuous life, wherein true manhood consists.   In making this classification, Aristotle
is taking into account the constitution of society as he
finds it about him, rather than the growth of institutions as historic inquiry reveals it.   Indeed, a knowledge of the latter was beyond his reach.   He accordingly fails to distinguish between the institutions
whose succession paves the way for the city-state and
the later modifications of these that arise through the
reaction of the same.

Historical research shows us that the earliest of
human associations is, indeed, the household—not,
however, the household as we understand it, but the
patriarchal family, consisting of persons related, or
supposed to, be related, to each other by blood, and
governed by its oldest member.   On the other hand,
it shows us that this is not something prior to and
different from the village community, but something
identical with it, at least among peoples who have
passed from the nomadic, to the settled, mode of life.
Now, one most important fact about the patriarchal
family is, that it is, above all, a religious community,
held together by religious ties.   In saying that it is
held together by blood-ties, and again by religious ties,
we are not making inconsistent or contradictory state-
ments : the blood-ties are religious ties, and all religious ties are originally blood-ties.   This is a fact
fraught with such momentous and all-pervasive results that we must dwell upon it at some length.

The patriarchal family consists of two main divisions : (1) its human members, (2) its brute members; and the former of these is again subdivided into two: (*a*) living members, (*b*) dead members. All these are held together by what may be called, indifferently, a blood-tie or a life-tie. In a word, the whole family is supposed to be instinct with a common life or blood, and, since it is upon the vigor of this life that the well-being of the whole and of the parts depends, every effort is made to strengthen it. With this view, from time to time a member of the family, usually a brute member, is put to death, and its flesh partaken of by all the human members, living and dead. Such is the origin of sacrifice, whose original purpose was to bind together into a strong, saving unity of life all the members, visible and invisible, of a family. The portion assigned to the latter was either poured, in the form of blood, upon the stone in which they were supposed to reside, or burned upon it in the shape of flesh or fat, so that they might inhale it in the form of vapor. Such is the origin of the altar, which was originally nothing else than a stone in which the life of an ancestor was supposed to reside, and on which, therefore, his share of the sacrificial meal was placed in such a form that he could enjoy it.* And this brings vividly before us the no-

---

* Of course, a share in the sacrificial meal was not the only thing that the invisible members of the household received. A portion of everything that was eaten or drunk was presented to them ; but a clear distinction was always drawn between sacrifices and offerings, at least among the Aryan and Semitic peoples. Among the Hebrews the distinction was felt to be so great that Abel, who offered a *sacrifice*, was said to have been accepted by God, while Cain, who presented an *offering*, was re-

4

tions entertained by those primitive households with
regard to the abode and the mode of life of their departed ancestors. It was supposed not only that these
were still present with the household, and that they
were deeply interested in its affairs, but also that its
welfare depended largely upon their favor, and their
happiness upon the actions and fortunes of its living
members.* It is very difficult for us in these days to
enter into such a conception of life and its relations
as this; but, unless we do, so we shall utterly fail to
understand not only ancient Greek life and education,
but also the whole life of the ancient world. That life
was, to its very core, permeated with religion, that
is, with a sense of dependence upon a unity of life
with the invisible lives of departed ancestors. To

---

jected (see Heb. xi, 4, and cf. Gen. iv, 4); and indeed it is frequently referred to in both the Old and New Testaments (see
Psalms, xl, 6; Heb. v, 1; viii, 3; ix, 9). In a fragment of Æschylus (156, Dind.), we find the same distinction made:

> " Alone of all the gods, Death loves not *gifts ;*
> Nay, nor with *sacrifice* nor drink poured out
> Canst thou accomplish aught with him."

It is a curious and significant fact that the sacrifice of Christ,
as viewed in Christian theology, accomplishes precisely what the
very earliest sacrifices were supposed to do : it binds men into
unity with each other and with their invisible Father. If sin
be regarded as a falling away from this unity, we can easily
understand that "it is the blood that maketh atonement by
reason of the life" (Lev. xvii, 11), and that "apart from shed-
ding of blood there is no remission" (Heb. ix, 22).

* This early belief in the presence of deceased ancestors in
the living household finds a striking illustration in the tombs
of ancient Etruria. These are fitted up exactly like the houses
of the living, with every convenience for a comfortable, or even
luxurious, existence.

maintain this unity was the supreme end of life, determining all action and all abstention from action. Remembering that these ghostly ancestors were the earliest gods,* we may say that the primitive household consisted of gods, men, and animals, bound together by a common life, and that its weal was conceived to depend upon the perfect integrity of this life. When a man died, his life was supposed to pass from his body, with which it had merely an accidental connection, into something else more durable—a stone, a rock, a tree, a spring, which then became at once sacred (*kadosh, ἱερά, sacra, taboo*). This, indeed, is the very meaning of " sacred." The actions performed by the living household with reference to these sacred objects constituted worship, whose sole aim was to preserve and strengthen the life of the whole.

We can now see how not only the vegetable but also the mineral world came to be regarded as sharing in the life of the household, and therefore as claiming an interest or respect quite different from that due to their material usefulness. We can also see how religion, in its earliest stages, assumed the forms of fetichism and animism, and how the feeling that a common life animated the entire household, with its animal, vegetable, and mineral surroundings, would, in course of time, develop into pantheism. But this

---

* There is much discussion at the present day as to whether the earliest gods were ghosts of ancestors or powers of nature personified. The question is really a vain one, since it credits primitive men with conceptions and distinctions to which they were entire strangers. The earliest gods were both ghosts and powers of nature, in this sense, that the powers of nature were conceived as being of the same nature as the life in man.

was a late result, possible only when men had arrived at a conception of the whole, or universe (τὸ πᾶν). The interests of primitive men were much narrower, being confined entirely to the household. What shared in its life or blood they regarded with sympathy; everything else with antipathy. "Friend" and "foe" meant originally kindred and alien.*

But the notion that the blood-tie could be strengthened by participation in the life of a sacrificed animal easily passed into the notion that it might be created by the same means. This paved the way, not only for the admission of members of one household into another, but even for the union of two or more entire households, a thing which the need of self-defence must often have suggested and rendered necessary. But the union of two households meant, not merely the coalescence of their living members into a new social whole, but also and primarily an alliance of their invisible members and a conjunction of the acts of worship performed to them; it meant, in a word, the union of two religions. But, inasmuch as the divinities of each household were attached to certain objects and localities, this would have been a matter of considerable difficulty, had there been no new conception to help it out. But such a conception there was. The notion that particular objects, stones,

---

* It is easy to see how from the word *freo*, signifying *to regard as kin*, should come the words *friend, free*; A. S. *frea* and *freo* (honored man and woman, lord and lady; cf. Arab. *sāhib*, meaning both friend and lord); Ger., *froh, fröhlich* (merry), etc.; and how from *feo* (*feog*), *to regard as an alien*, we should get *foe, fiend, feud*; Scot., *fey* (doomed to death; Isl., *feigr*); Ger., *feig* (cowardly), *faugh*; Scot., *feech*, etc.

trees, springs, etc., were endowed with life naturally widened out into the notion that each department of visible nature was so endowed, a process which would be greatly hastened in cases where families were forced to leave their old homes, and therewith the objects of worship supposed to be animated by the lives of their ancestors. Instead, now, of worshiping the particular rock or stone, they worshiped a mountain, or even the earth owned by them; instead of the particular tree, all trees, whole groves, or even the expanse of heaven; instead of the particular spring, all springs, streams, and finally all water.* In this way ancestor-worship passed, in the most natural way, into nature-worship.

Thus the advance from ancestor-worship to nature-worship corresponds to an advance in social development—an advance from the village community to what the Greeks called a phratry (φράτρα or φρατρία), the Latins a *curia*, and the Germans a *hundred*. The process was a slow one, and in neither case did the new supersede the old; it was merely superimposed

---

* In the *Rig-Veda* (vii, 34, 23) we read: "May the mountains, the waters, the generous plants, and heaven, may the earth with the trees, and the two worlds, protect our wealth!" In the *Avesta* (Yasna, lxviii, 3) we read: "We sacrifice to the sea Vouru-Kasha, and to all waters upon earth, whether standing or running, or waters of the well, or spring waters which perennially flow, or the drippings of the rains, or the irrigations of canals." How easily the notion of an overarching tree passed into that of the overarching heaven, may be seen in the case of the Zoroastrian *Harvisptokhm* (see Sacred Books of the East, vol. iv, p. 54, n. 2), in the Norse *Yggdrasil* (see Simrock, *Handbuch der deutschen Mythologie*, pp. 32 *sqq.*), and in such Greek phrases as δένδρεα οὐρανομήκεα (Herod., ii, 138), ἐλάτης οὐράνιον ἄκρον κλάδον (Eurip., *Bacch.*, 1064).

upon it. While the ancestor-worships remained the religions of the households composing the phratry, nature-worship became the religion of the phratry in its corporate capacity. This change was a most important one for civilization, involving far-reaching consequences. Previously, all worship had been a family matter, conducted by the family-head or patriarch, at the family shrines, that is, near the objects supposed to be animated by the lives of their ancestors. Now, it became a public matter, conducted at the common meeting place of the households, by a person specially chosen for the purpose, in honor of beings attached to no special material objects, but present in large portions of nature. The meeting-place now assumed a sacred character—became, in fact, a temple (τέμενος, ἱερόν); the new official was a priest (ἱερεύς); the new worship expressed the new unity by relating the participating households to common ancestors older than those worshiped by them separately. As to the last fact, it was but natural that the new social union should seem possible only as representing the recovery of long-forgotten blood-ties; for in those days all friendly relations were conceived as blood-relations, as indeed they are still among peoples in the village-community stage of culture. The new union took a name generally, though not always, plural in form. The singular of this was looked upon as the name of the founder of the community, who was now represented as the son of the divinity selected as the patron of that community.

In this new social union we find the beginnings of many things that afterward assumed momentous proportions—e. g., (1) of the separation of patriarchal and

priestly functions; * (2) of public worship; (3) of the belief that men sprang from nature-divinities; (4) of social, as distinct from household duties and relations; (5) of the substitution of a land-bond for the blood-bond, as the principle of social union. In this widening of life the important thing to observe is, that life remained essentially religious, that the new social unities were religious associations. Through the gradual superposition of the land-bond, however, upon the blood-bond, social religion came to be connected with territorial limits instead of with blood-relationship.†
Hence we frequently find divinities named after districts—e. g., Artemis Munychia, Artemis Brauronia (who had a temple on the Athenian acropolis), etc. Hence also we find growing up alongside the sense of family or kin the sense of country or fatherland

---

* This, which was the germ of the separation between Church and State, seems to have taken place in Greece and Latium very early, so that the priests never formed a ruling class possessing civil power. It was otherwise among the Hebrews, with whom the priests formed a kind of caste, which at all times exercised great social influence, and in the end absorbed all political power. Their ideal was a "kingdom of priests" (Exod. xix, 6). It is curious to find that Moses, when he unites the households of his people, finds it necessary to cement that union by the sanction of a new divinity, Jahweh, who has appeared to him in a burning bush. This divinity at once takes a position above the old Elohim or household divinities, who soon lose their individualities and sink into a being who seems indifferent as to number, and is ultimately identified with Jahweh. See the curious passage in Gen. xviii, where Jahweh appears to Abraham as three men !

† This relation of a god to the land was expressed in Hebrew by the word Baal. See Robertson Smith, *Relig. of the Semites*, p. 93.

(πατρίς, πατρὶς γαῖα), and the notion that membership
in the society held together by that bond involves possession of a share in that land.   It was on the basis of
this notion that there came to be introduced that distinction, so important in its consequences, between
nobles, or possessors, and commons, or non-possessors
—between eorlas and ceorlas, as the old English said.

How this came about seems clear enough. As the
sense of the land-bond strengthened, that of the blood-
bond proportionately weakened, so that the old patriarchal families, though still acknowledging a blood-
connection, and giving it expression in sacrifices,
gradually broke up into monogamic households in
the modern sense, which stood in direct relation to the
phratry. At the same time the land which had previously been held in common by the members of the
patriarchal families was gradually broken up into lots,
which became the private property of the new households.   Thus private property in land and the monogamic family have their origin in the same social change.
But in course of time, as families multiplied, without
any corresponding increase of territory, a certain number of them were forced to go without land and betake
themselves to handicrafts, fishing, and the like.   But
as membership in the phratry had come to be regarded
as depending upon possession of land, these landless
families occupied an inferior position, becoming in
fact dependent upon the landed proprietors. Thus
society was divided up into two classes, whose interests
were not always found to coincide—classes which we
may term nobles (εὐγενεῖς) and commons (ἀγενεῖς).

But inasmuch as a superior class has always difficulty in maintaining its privileges, it was natural that

the nobles should combine in order to maintain theirs.
In doing this they founded the third political institution, the city-state, which was originally nothing more
than a stronghold of nobles with their dependents,
making common cause to hold in subjection the less
privileged class. The better to accomplish their purpose, they chose a head or king, surrounded their
stronghold with walls, and chose gods to cement their
union.* And what is the principle of this union?
We have seen that in the family the bond was blood,
in the phratry or hundred, land. In the city-state it
was nobility, which, though originally based upon
property in land, came, in course of time, to imply a
good deal more. Aristotle rightly defines "nobility"
as "ancient wealth and worth" (ἡ γὰρ εὐγένειά ἐστιν
ἀρχαῖος πλοῦτος καὶ ἀρετή, *Polit.*, iv, 8) ; and the worth
came finally to be the more important element.

With the establishment of the city, an enormous
change took place in the relations of society. A clear
line was now drawn between gentle and simple, between citizens and rustics (πολῖται and δημόται). There
now came into existence a leisure-class which regarded
itself as having no duties except to govern the other
classes and cultivate worth (ἀρετή), a term which,
though it connoted different things at different times,
always denoted those qualities which enable a man to
govern. The ground was now prepared in which the
higher manifestations of humanity—art, science, philosophy, statesmanship, ethical religion—might grow

---

* Such gods were called πολιοῦχοι; cf. πολιεύς, πολιάς, etc.
It is curious to find that these epithets, like φράτριος, are confined
to Zeus and Athena.

and flourish; for, strange as it may seem, these are well-nigh impossible without a class of men which manages to have its material wants supplied by another class. But, in spite of these momentous changes, the constitution of society still remained religious. During the phratrial period, indeed, the original meaning of sacrificial rites had been forgotten, and numerous myths invented to explain them; but they still continued to be performed with ever-increasing pomp and circumstance, though with a new aim. This aim was conditioned by the new views entertained with regard to the gods. We have seen that in the patriarchal period the gods (if we may so call them) were the imagined ghosts of ancestors, residing in special natural objects; and that in the phratrial period they were identified with the powers of nature. In what we may now call the political period they came more and more to be thought of as beings standing above nature and guiding it according to moral ideas; in fact, they become moral gods. This is perhaps the most momentous change that ever took place in human history, being, indeed, the change from the natural to the spiritual man. When sacrifices were offered to such gods, they were offered as pledges of loyalty, expressions of gratitude, or propitiations for disloyalty, and hence were usually accompanied with prayers for benignity and aid.

With the city-state and its moral gods, Greek social progress reached its highest point. Some steps indeed were taken toward the foundation of a nation in the establishment of the great periodical gatherings at Olympia, Delphi, Nemea, and other places; but beyond this they never went. All attempts to go further proved uniformly abortive. No confederation even ever included the whole of Greece. On the other hand, no sooner was the city-state well established than it began to react upon the institutions which had paved the way for it, modifying them in such a way as to render them its organs. In treating of this reactive process we shall direct our attention to Athens, (1) because her history may be regarded as typical, and (2) because it is better known to us than any other.

From the earliest times of which we have any history, Attica, the territory ruled by the nobles (εὐπατρίδαι) having their seat in Athens, was systematically divided, and it is obvious that no such division could have taken place until a central organizing power was constituted. The earliest division so established seems to have been into tribes, corresponding to social status and profession, but in part also to territorial divisions. Later on each tribe seems to have been divided into three trittyes or ridings, corresponding pretty closely, if not altogether, to the old phratries; and later still, each trittys into four naucraries or fiscal districts. Just *when* these arrangements were made, is not at all clear. I am inclined to think that the first, and perhaps the second, were due to Theseus, while the third was not introduced till about the time of Solon.*

---

* The four ancient tribes, said to have been introduced by Cecrops, were named (1) Geleontes, or nobles; (2) Hopletes, or warriors; (3) Ægicoreis, or shepherds; and (4) Argadeis, or craftsmen. Theseus is said to have divided the people into *three* classes: (1) Eupatridai, or nobles; (2) Geomoroi, or farmers; and (3) Demiourgoi, or craftsmen. But it is clear that if Attica

This caste system, as we may fairly enough call it, continued down to the time of the revolution of Clisthenes. This founder of Athenian democracy, with the aid of the populace, broke up the old caste tribes and formed ten new ones, in each of which all the castes were placed on an equal footing, and into which many new citizens, excluded from the old tribes, were admitted. These tribes, which corresponded to no local divisions, were each subdivided into three ridings (τριττύες) and ten village-communities, named, as far as possible, after the reputed founders of the old patriarchal families, and arranged in such a way that neighboring demes belonged to different tribes. The tribes themselves were named after ancient Attic heroes.

The important feature in this new division was that it was purely political, no longer religious, as the old divisions had been. As Aristotle, in his recently discovered *Constitution of Athens*, tells us, "the clans (patriarchal families), phratries, and priesthoods Clisthenes allowed to continue in their hereditary forms" (cap. xxi). Thus, for the first time in history, we have a country in which the citizens live under two distinct dispensations—the one religious and the other political; for as soon as the new division was established, the old lost its political features and significance, and became purely religious. It is true that

---

was not united under one government until the time of Theseus, no division into tribes could have taken place till then; and it seems to me that Eupatridai is only a common name for Geleontes and Hopletes, while Geomoroi and Demiourgoi are only modern names for Ægicoreis and Argadeis respectively. The tripartite division plays no part in Attic political history. The four tribes lasted till B. C. 509.

the two dispensations did not stand unrelated (that would have been impossible); but they belonged to two different orders of ideas, and exercised distinct functions. The old religious dispensation assumed men to be held together in society by a blood-bond. This had partly given way, first, to a land-bond, and, later, to a worth-bond. Each of these bonds was supposed to be presided over by a deity. When the worth-bond was reached, its presiding divinity was necessarily conceived as a spiritual and moral being, and the way was paved for organizing the whole of society by means of a spiritual bond. This was done, to a very large extent, in the democratic constitution of Clisthenes. In fact, the success of democracy meant the triumph of the spiritual bond over the material bond, which had been the basis of the old religious constitutions; and though these were not completely broken up, their sphere of action was confined to religious observances. It was, in great measure, to this separation between Church and State, as we may call it, that Athens owed that wonderful development of material and spiritual power which followed upon the revolution of Clisthenes.

We have thus briefly traced the growth of those institutions in which Greek life successively embodied its social ideals: (1) the patriarchal family or clan; (2) the phratry; (3) the city-state, which, rising gradually to a spiritual ideal, organized, first, the tribe, the riding, and the naucrary, and subsequently the tribe, the riding, and the village (δῆμος). We have seen that the social bond of the city-state, the highest of Greek social institutions, was worth (ἀρετή). If now we bear in mind that at all periods of Greek history the ideal of life was social, that the individual and the citizen were never distinguished, we can see how that which formed the social bond of the city-state became the ideal of life for the individual, and consequently the goal of education.

And so, indeed, it was. In Greece the ideal of life and education concentrated itself in the one conception of worth. It is true that this conception changed its content as time went on; but it always connoted those qualities which mark the worthy member of society. For the reason that it had come to be the social bond only as the result of a long process, it could never quite belie its origin, and hence never came to mean simply and solely moral worth. It always contained something of the old blood- and land-bond. Rarely, indeed, and only in the decline of Greek life, was worth attributed to a man, unless he could claim noble birth and landed wealth. It was this fact that conditioned the nature of Athenian democracy, and that constitutes the great distinction between it and the democracies of modern times, which have altogether disowned both the blood- and the land-bond.

When the Greeks first come before us in the pages of Homer, they have already, for the most part, reached the political stage marked by the city-state. Theseus, the founder of the Athenian constitution, has already been dead for a generation. But though even in those early days a considerable advance had been made toward a moral conception of the gods, yet it took many generations before this assumed definite form in contradistinction to the old materialistic notions, and many more before its full significance revealed itself in the

organization of society and in education, which always
bore a close relation to that organization. When it
did finally become the organizing force in life, and
expressed itself in democracy, it seemed at first to
draw men away from religion altogether, the reason
being that religion, or the observances of religion, had
remained at the older point of view, while the present
social force occupied the new. The gulf thus opened
between religion and political life the Greeks never
succeeded in closing. Their efforts to do so expressed
themselves in that wonderful product of the Greek
mind, philosophy, which was at bottom nothing but
an attempt to find a justification for worth, as the
social bond, in the constitution of the universe, or the
nature of the gods; we may perhaps say, to bring the
gods and their world up to the new moral idea. But
while the best men were trying to embody the new
bond in life, the two older bonds—blood and wealth—
were fighting for supremacy; and in the struggle between them Greece perished, leaving her ideal to be
realized elsewhere. And it has not yet been realized
fully. From the days of Clisthenes to our own, philosopher and priest and statesman have vainly endeavored to reconcile religion and politics, until now, at
last, we have come to congratulate ourselves upon
what seems their permanent separation. But reconciled they will undoubtedly one day be, when we come
to understand wherein human worth really consists,
and to see that it is, and must be, the sole end of all
human institutions.*

---

* It is curious to note that, in the breaking up of the solidarity between religion and politics, the Greeks under Clisthenes

Worth, then—the worth of the individual as a member of society—was the Greek ideal of life and education. Of course, the content of this ideal differed, with the demands of society, from generation to generation. In early times, when the city-state was fighting for existence against enemies at home and abroad, worth necessarily consisted in practical ability—in being able to see, and in public to express, what needed to be done, and in being prompt and effective in the doing of it. Such is the worth which we find aimed at by the heroes in Homer, by Agamemnon, Achilles, and the rest. Of course, the Greeks could hardly conceive, either then or at any time, that such virtue could be attained by any man who was not well-born and possessed of wealth; still, these advantages were by no means conceived as constituting worth or public usefulness, as they have sometimes been since.

Later on, when the social organization became more secure, when the citizens (πολῖται) were not obliged to devote all their energies to defending it, when they enjoyed a certain amount of leisure which they felt the necessity of occupying worthily, new elements entered into the conception of worth. If a man would deserve the title of worthy now, he must be able, not only to do his part in the practical and necessary business of life, but also to fill the time gained from business with occupations which should be ends in

---

went the one way and founded a purely political institution, while the Hebrews, under Isaiah, went the other, and laid the foundations of a Church. Christianity has sought in vain to unite these two institutions in a Kingdom of Heaven, wherein Hebrew prophecy and Greek philosophy shall supplement each other.

themselves, looking to nothing beyond. Such time,
and the occupations which belonged to it, were called
by the Greeks διαγωγή (*diagōgē*), a word for which our
language offers no equivalent. We must dwell upon
it, and the thought expressed by it, for a moment.

To the cultivated Greek, life divided itself sharply
into two portions, one to be devoted to means, and the
other to ends. Under means was included whatever
related to practical life, the earning of a livelihood,
politics, war, education, religious observances, etc.;
under ends, what were called the occupations of the
Muses—that is, fine art, science, and philosophy.
These, indeed, were the ends to which all other occupations were but means. The enjoyment of them
was designated by the term διαγωγή, which must be
clearly distinguished, not only from practical life, but
also from mere play or amusement. Play was regarded
as a mere preparation for practical work, therefore as
a means to a means : διαγωγή, on the contrary, was the
end and aim of practical work. This distinction conditioned the whole of Greek life and education. It is
to be found in Homer * ; it passed over from Greek
thought into historical Christianity, and became a
powerful factor in it. When the Middle Age, following the Neoplatonists, said that the contemplative life

---

* Odysseus (*Odyss.*, ix, 5 *sqq.*) says : "For I declare there is
no more delightful *end* than when festivity takes possession of a
whole people, and the guests in the palace listen to the minstrel,
sitting in rows ; and the tables beside them are loaded with
bread and meats, and the cup-bearer, drawing wine from the
mixing-bowl, carries it round and pours it into the cups. This
seems to my heart to be something very beautiful." To this
every Greek heart would have responded.

was the goal of the practical, it was only repeating the Greek doctrine in slightly different words.

Bearing in mind now that the ideal of Greek life was worth, and that this meant capability in all the spheres of activity, whether practical or "diagogic," we can have little difficulty in seeing what the character and limits of the education which sought to impart such capability must have been. It is obvious that, just as the spheres of activity were different at different times and places, so likewise were the systems of education. In primitive times, when life was mainly practical, education was a preparation for practice. As life became more and more diagogic, education followed in the same direction. Again, while some states like Athens made room for and encouraged diagogic life, others, like Sparta, opposed it, and remained almost completely within the practical sphere. It followed that the Athenian and Spartan schemes of education were widely different.

As in dealing with Greek education our chief attention will be directed to Athens, we may consider for a moment the extent and divisions of the Athenian citizen's range of activity.

Every citizen was a member, *first*, of a family (οἶκος) ; *second*, of a township (δῆμος) ; *third*, of a phratry (φρατρία) ; *fourth*, of a riding (τριττύς) ; *fifth*, of a tribe (φυλή) ; and *sixth*, of the state (πόλις) ; and each of these relations involved special duties.* As

---

* This of course refers to post-Clisthenean times. In earlier days every citizen was a member of a clan (γένος) and of a naucrary (ναυκραρία). Clisthenes deprived the clans of all political significance, by admitting to citizenship many who did not belong to them, while the naucraries he entirely abolished.

member of a family, a man had duties as priest, as husband, as father, and as owner of property and slaves; as member of a township, he had to do his part in everything that related to the property, the worship, and the internal laws of the town, as well as in everything that had to do with its relations to the superior institutions; as member of a phratry, he had to participate in certain religious rites, and to aid in protecting the state against the unlawful assumption by spurious children of the rights of citizenship. His membership in a riding and a tribe merely determined the company in which he should act in his various relations as member of the state. These relations involved duties of three kinds besides those of religion: (1) administrative, (2) judicial, (3) military. It is needless to say that these were regarded as his supreme duties. It thus appears that the Athenian citizen who wished to claim the honor (τιμή) of worth, had to be a good husband, a good father, a good property-owner, a good town-member, a good state-officer, a good judge, a good soldier, and, along with all this, a pious worshiper of the gods of every institution of which he was a member. These were his practical duties, and in early times were all that was expected of him. If he failed in any of them he could be reached by the arm of the law. But in proportion as diagogic life became possible and was aimed at, other duties which the law could not enforce were added to these by the power of public opinion. It then became incumbent upon a man to be able to take an intelligent part in all those social avocations with which men sought to occupy their leisure hours in a worthy and godlike way, by giving free and self-sufficient expression to their own noblest nature. These avocations consisted chiefly in feasting, in the enjoyment of the various products of the liberal arts, and in serious conversation. In the first the animal nature, in the second the emotional nature, in the third the intellect, found free expression. It was altogether characteristic of the Greek, and particularly of the Athenian, to see that in that activity which formed the end of life no part of his nature should be neglected. We must not forget that to him feasting bore the same relation to ordinary eating and drinking that the "fine" arts bore to the useful. He had not forgotten that in the "good old time" the worship of the gods consisted chiefly of feasting. For these diagogic occupations, no less than for the practical ones, an education was needed, and indeed such an education formed an essential part of the life-preparation of every Athenian who laid any claim to worth.

Such, then, was the origin and nature of the Greek ideal of life—the ideal which at every stage determined the character of Greek education.

CHAPTER III.

GREEK EDUCATION BEFORE THE RISE OF PHILOSOPHY.

THE history of Greek education—that is, of education in free Greece—is divided into two fairly distinct periods by two contemporaneous events, the conflict with Persia and the rise of philosophy. In the period previous to these events education was for the most part a preparation for practical life; in the period succeeding them it aimed more and more at being a preparation for diagogic life. In what is called the Hellenistic period, when Greece was no longer free, the latter tendency altogether gained the upper hand, for the reason mainly that practical life, in the old Greek sense, no longer existed. I purpose in the present lecture to deal with the education of the first period, with what Aristophanes in his *Clouds* calls the "Old Education."

The period in question begins for us with the social condition presented in the Homeric poems. Already the Greeks have passed beyond the patriarchal and phratrial stages of civilization and have developed the city-state and the tribe.* Notwith-

---

* The phratry (φρήτρη) and the tribe (φῦλον) are both mentioned in *Iliad* ii, 362–3; but this does not belong to the oldest part of the work.

standing this, there exists as yet nothing resembling
a school. Whatever education there is, not only forms
a preparation for practical life, but is also gained in
practical life—in the house, the agora, the council, the
field, the camp. The growing boy, as soon as he passes
out of the hands of nurses, spends his time in the company of men, learning by precept and example to do
what they do, and discovering by means of his own
wits why they do it. At first he imitates them in play
with his fellows; but as soon as his powers permit, he
takes serious part in their occupations. It was, indeed,
the aim of the Greek, at all periods, to render his sons
independent members of society at as early an age as
possible.

It is not easy for us, with our mediæval notions of the
value of school education, to think that a man could
be really educated who had never heard of a school;
but this is due to the fact that we find it difficult to
realize the conditions of early Greek life. Our lives
are so hedged round with conventionalities, which in a
thousand ways sunder us and prevent us from sharing
our spiritual wealth with each other, that we can scarce-
ly conceive a state of things in which such conventionalities hardly existed, when every member of a state
looked upon every other as a brother; * when men lived
mostly in the open air and in hourly contact with each
other, conversing, playing, hunting, worshiping, delib-

---

* Macaulay was guilty of no exaggeration when he said:

"The Romans were like brothers
In the brave days of old."

Compare Dante's bitter reflections on his own time, Purga-
tory, vi, 76 *sqq.*

erating, drilling, fighting, in fact doing everything together; when there were no titles—no "Mr." even—
no family names, no rules of etiquette, nothing to prevent any one from addressing, or even "pumping,"
anybody he met.   Under such circumstances the experience and accomplishments of each could not fail
to be communicated to all, especially as a continual
rivalry was going on, which greatly stimulated the
pursuit of excellence.   This rivalry, or tendency to
competition, was a strongly marked trait of the Greek
character at all periods.   To it were due not only such
institutions as the great games, but likewise much of
what is best in Greek science, philosophy, and art.   But
the horizon of the early Greek was not bounded by the
limits of his own state.   War, trade, and piracy* were
continually bringing him into contact with foreigners
and foreign wares.†   His captives became his slaves,
and had many tales to tell of far-off lands and strange
customs and gods.‡   And then there was the omni-
present, ever-welcome wandering minstrel, who, like
Odysseus, "had seen the cities of many men and
known their minds," in whose songs were stored up
the history of past ages and the descriptions of distant
lands, and who dispensed his lore in the form best
suited to hold the memory, to fill the imagination,
and to influence the conduct.   Thus the Homeric
Greeks, though perhaps not one in a thousand of

---

* "Krieg, Handel und Piraterie,
   Dreieinig sind sie, nicht zu trennen."—*Faust*, Pt. ii.

† The objects recently unearthed at Mycenæ, Spata, and
other places show how much foreign art was introduced into
Greece even in pre-Homeric times.

‡ Witness the case of Eumæus in the *Odyssey*.

them could read or write, were, in the very truest
sense, educated people, and their education was all the
better, fresher, and more serviceable, that it was gained
amid the concrete relations of actual life, and laid hold
of the whole living human being—his affections and
his will, no less than his memory and his intelligence.
There is nothing that delights us in the Homeric Greek
more than his perfect simplicity, directness, undisguised
feeling, and natural freedom from palaver and senti-
mentality.   And it is not difficult to see that he owed
these charming qualities, which must forever make
him attractive, to the character of his education, which
from first to last kept him in the closest contact with
the facts of life—domestic, social, and political.   It
was in the small city-states of Greece that the finer elements of human nature—devoted, unselfish friendship,
domestic purity, respect for women, reverence for law,
loyalty to institutions—were first able clearly to manifest themselves.   It may well be doubted whether at
any subsequent period of their history the Greeks were
as well educated, in the true sense of that word, as
they were in the days of Homer.   No other period has
given us men equal to Hector and Achilles, or women
equal to Penelope and Nausicaa.

The age described by Homer was one of great energy and brilliancy in all directions—one of those ages
in which men and women seem to attain their full
stature.   But ere he came upon the scene it was drawing to a close.   It was succeeded by what, by way of
contrast, may be called a " dark age "—an age of social
unrest, of tribal migrations, of rapid dissolution of old
ties and institutions, and slow and painful establishment of new ones.   During this period, which lasted

for over three hundred years—a period of which neither history, poetry, nor archæology has left us any connected or adequate account—the older civilization, which seems to have reached its culmination under the empire of the "wide-ruling Agamemnon," faded away into a gigantic myth,* thus passing gradually from the hands of History into those of Poetry. About the middle of the eighth century B. C., Greece reappears in the pages of history and in the discoveries of archæology; but she is a very different Greece from that which vanished three centuries before. She appears now as a cluster of independent and mutually hostile states, each fighting over again the battle for existence, and each claiming for itself a share in the mythic renown of the heroic past, which Homer has already made forever glorious. She rises, as it were, from her grave, with Homer in her hand, and Homer henceforth largely shapes her destinies. Her people are henceforth a "people of the book." † It would hardly be possible to overestimate the importance of this fact.

A people with a book is something very different from a people without a book. A book not only enriches by its contents the intellectual and imaginative life of a people, but it divides their world into two

---

* See Goethe's splendid description of this in the opening of the fourth act of the second part of *Faust*.

† *Ahlu 'l-kitabi*, as Muhammad called the Jews, Christians, and Sabæans. It is true that the Greeks were never a "people of the book" in the same sense that the Jews and Christians are; that is, they never made a book the authoritative law of their lives; nevertheless, it seems plain that Homer exerted a paramount influence upon their whole spiritual development.

parts—one real, the other ideal; one that is, the other
that ought to be. The old idyllic immediateness and
joyous satisfaction with the present are gone. The
actual is found to be partial, and has to be supplemented by an imagined past, thrown as a possibility
upon the vacant screen of the future. Hence a strain
of pathos, forming a discord, runs through the whole
of life, becoming more and more sensible as time goes
on.* When it becomes apparent that this discord can
not be resolved in every-day practical life, an attempt
is made to supplement this by another kind of life, in
which it may be resolved. If this is conceived as possible in this world, there results an endeavor after what
the Greeks called diagogic life; if not, there is born
the conception of a heaven, hid from mortal eyes in
the depths of the unseen.

Among the Greeks the result of the separation between real and ideal life, consequent upon the possession of a book, was an endeavor after diagogic life;
and it was in seeking to realize this that they devoted
themselves to art, science, and philosophy, the social
enjoyment of which constituted διαγωγή.† The effort
in this direction naturally began with the recital of the
poems of Homer. This called into existence a class of

---

* This pathos, which is almost entirely lacking in Homer, is
apparent from the first in the authors of what we may call the
Renaissance. It is quite marked even in Hesiod, whose works
open the new period. The elegiac and lyric poets are full of it
—Callinus, Theognis, Alcman, Simonides, etc.

† When Aristotle divides the sciences into practical and
theoretical, he means that the former find their application in
practical life, while the latter serve for διαγωγή. Theory (θεωρία)
is the occupation even of the gods, who enjoy perpetual διαγωγή.

men known as rhapsodes (ῥαψωδοί). The first of these
is said, and with apparent truth, to have been Hesiod,
whose own works long held a place beside those of
Homer. The rhapsodes differed from the old minstrels
(ἀοιδοί), or epic poet-singers, in three ways: (1) they
merely recited the works of others: they were not
(usually at least) poets; (2) they gave no musical ac-
companiment; (3) they frequently accompanied their
recitations with a commentary, or exposition.* In
fact, they bore very much the same relation to the
epic poets that the scribes (sopherim) among the
Jews did to the prophets; and, indeed, the prophets
of the Greeks were their poets (vates). But the poems
of Homer and Hesiod did not long remain the only
occupation of διαγωγή. There soon arose poems of a
new order—no longer epic, but elegiac, lyric, and
gnomic—and these were accompanied with new kinds
of music, more varied and also more complicated than
the old. The various kinds of poetry, with their different accompaniments, were included under the common term music (μουσική), i. e., Muses' work, whose
patrons were the Muses. These, with the gods whose
company they kept—Dionysus, Apollo, Hermes—thus
became the divinities of διαγωγή, which, like the rest
of life, was essentially religious.

But with the division of life into two parts—one
real, the other ideal—there came a division of men
into two classes: one whose life was confined to the
real; the other, which could rise into the ideal, the

---

* See Plato's *Ion* and Isocrates' *Panath.*, p. 239. Hence
Heraclitus could say of the people of his time: " Hesiod is the
teacher of most " (Frag. xxxv, Bywater).

crown and end of life (τὸ τέλος).* The latter alone
were supposed to be gentlemen (ἐλευθέριοι); and thus
gentlemanliness came to be associated with elegant
leisure.† Again, as διαγωγή came to occupy a larger
and larger place in life, so its presiding deities came
more and more to be worshiped. But these deities,
one and all, were, if we may so speak, deities of the
unseen and ideal, and hence their worship always contained a mystic element. This is especially true of
Dionysus and the Muses; and it is clear that the
whole mystic or Orphic tendency which we find in
post-Homeric—we might fairly say, post-Renaissance
—Greek literature, from Hesiod ‡ onward, is closely
connected with their worship. But mysticism in religion always implies a strong reflective and pantheistic tendency in thought, and this shows itself, not
only in Hesiod, but still more clearly in the so-called
Orphic poetry, some of which is probably of the same
date. It was this tendency that, in course of time,
took form in Greek philosophy, which was never quite
able to emancipate itself from pantheism.

It would be easy to trace to διαγωγή the origin, not
only of philosophy, but also of all the things with
which cultured leisure was occupied—art, symposia,
etc.—as well as of those later philosophic societies or

---

* Aristotle objects to young people's being allowed to enjoy
διαγωγή, on the ground that "the crown of perfection belongs
not to the imperfect" (οὐδὲ γὰρ ἀτελεῖ προσήκει τέλος, Pol. viii, 4).

† Τὸ καλὸν καὶ τὸ ἡδύ, the noble and the pleasant, the elements
of happiness, according to Aristotle.

‡ Hesiod himself stood in close relation to the famous seat
of the Muses on Mount Helicon. See the opening lines of the
Theogony and Works and Days, 656 sqq.

brotherhoods, which strove to make diagogic life permanent and "separate from the world" of practical
life. But the important points in the whole diagogic
tendency, and those which have a bearing on education, are these: (1) that it divided life into two distinct, though correlated, parts; (2) that it separated
men into two classes; (3) that it called into existence
the conception of a life which was an end in itself;
(4) that it strove to fill that life with enjoyments which
had no object beyond themselves, unless, indeed, it
might be to prepare for higher enjoyments of a similar
kind; and (5) that it caused such life to be regarded
as the only true and worthy life, the only life capable
of being eternal. It was long, indeed, before all these
results of the tendency completely manifested themselves; nevertheless, we must recognize its presence
and working from the days of Hesiod onward, if we
desire to follow intelligently the course of Greek education. From the time of Hesiod up to the rise of
philosophy proper the practical tendency still prevails
in life and education; after that the diagogic gradually gains the upper hand, until finally, in the Hellenistic period, it occupies the entire field. At present
we are dealing with the old period, in which the ideal
of worth still connoted, for the most part, only what
were called "political" virtues.* The only "theoretic" virtue it included was the power to enjoy poetry
and music—to *enjoy*, not to *produce*.

From the earliest times of which we have any his-

---

* When the two kinds of life were clearly distinguished in
consciousness, the corresponding virtues were distinguished as
political and theoretical (πολιτικαὶ καὶ θεωρητικαί).

torical record Greek education was divided into two parts: (1) Gymnastics for the body, and (2) Music for the soul. The soul in this connection does not include the intelligence, for it was long before the Greeks thought of providing any kind of education for it. Music was merely an exercise for the soul, intended to strengthen and harmonize its emotions, just as gymnastics strengthened and harmonized the bodily faculties. Both parts of education, therefore, were equally intended as a preparation for practical life, and so long as these constituted the whole of education, no schools, in the modern sense of the term, seem to have been found necessary. Young men could learn gymnastics and music, just as they did in Homer's time, by watching and imitating the exercises of their elders. Schools, in all probability, were introduced only when special provision had to be made for the intelligence—that is, when the intelligence had to acquire something that could not be learned in the ordinary course of life. This something was reading and writing—γράμματα (letters), as the Greeks said. Just at what time letters came to be regarded as an essential part of education is not quite clear; but it was probably not long before the year B. C. 600, which we may perhaps set down as the date of the earliest prose-composition. For some time before that they seem to have been used for commercial purposes, for inscriptions, and, by the rhapsodes and lyric singers, for recording poetical productions, which at that time had become too numerous to be carried in the memory. The fact that the "musicians" were the first persons who employed letters for literary purposes, combined with the other fact that they were always regarded in the light of public teachers, helps to explain how it came about that they were for many ages the sole teachers of letters. Letters, in fact, were considered a part of music, and thus it came to pass that all literature, no matter what its subject, was placed under the auspices of the Muses and their leader Apollo (hence Μουσαγέτης), who for this reason became the patron deities of schools.

At whatever date schools may have come into existence, it is certain that in the time of Solon, about B. C. 590, they were already in full operation in Athens, and that alongside of them there were regular institutions for physical training. Solon found it necessary to make laws, some of which are still extant, for both. A music school was called διδασκαλεῖον, and the master of it κιθαριστής (lute-player), while the school for physical training was called παλαίστρα (wrestling-ground) and its master παιδοτρίβης (boy-thresher or boy-kneader). Between the two schools the Athenian boy spent most of his day, from sunrise to sunset; and Solon had to make a law forbidding teachers to have their schools open before the former, or after the latter, of these hours.

Athenian boys, and Greek boys generally, went to school about the age of seven. Up to that time they remained at home with their sisters, under the charge of their mothers mostly, or of whatever nurses she might choose to appoint. Greek girls, except in Sparta and some Æolian cities, did not go to school at all. As long as education was meant to be merely a preparation for practical life, it was, of course, determined by the demands of that life. For a man practical life meant the life of a husband, father, and property owner, and of a member of a village, a phratry, and a state; for a woman it meant the life of a wife, mother, and housekeeper. Hence every effort was made to bring a boy as soon as possible into contact with public life, while a girl was rigidly excluded from it and confined to the home. It was only as diagogic education came into prominence that men and women met on a common ground outside the home; and even then the meeting was not accomplished without difficulty and moral confusion.

While children were under the care of their mothers and nurses, the first aim of the education imparted to them was to strengthen their bodies; the second, to inspire them with reverence for their elders; and the third, to fill their imaginations with pictures of heroic deeds drawn from the mythology or history of their race. With a view to the first, they were nourished on simple food, allowed plenty of sleep and open-air exercise, and inured, as far as possible, to heat and cold. They seem to have worn almost no clothing. With a view to the second, they were trained to habits of silence, obedience, and respectful demeanor in the presence of their parents. At table they ate only what was handed to them. With a view to the third, they were entertained with songs and stories about gods and goddesses, heroes and heroines—stories of which an abundant supply, expressed in poetic language, was to be found in the epics of Homer and the later cyclic poets, not to mention the folklore, which was abundant.

At the end of their seventh year boys were removed from the care of their mothers and nurses and sent to school. Going to school meant a great deal more in

those days than it usually means in ours. It meant the
beginning of an entirely new kind of life—viz., political
life. Greek schools were burgher-schools (*Bürger-
schulen*) in a very strict sense; and though the state
did not provide them or (in Athens at least) compel
any one to attend them, it oversaw them and used
them for its purposes—that is, for the training of
citizens in all political and social (that is, diagogic)
activities. In school, boys were thrown into a sort of
preparatory public life; for the music school and the
palæstra were to them what the agora and the gymnasium were to grown men : their daily life was spent in
them. Leaving home at daybreak, and with almost
no clothing, the boys, each accompanied by his pedagogue, assembled at some appointed spot, and thence
walked through the streets, in rank and file, to school.
It seems that freeborn boys and girls were not permitted to walk in the streets without attendants. The
pedagogue, usually an aged and worn-out slave, though
not expected to impart to his ward any literary instruction, nevertheless played a great part in his education,
being his guardian and monitor during the whole of
the time that he was not immediately under the eye of
his parents and teachers—that is, while he was on his
way to and from school and during his hours of recre-
ation and play, which were not short. There can be
little doubt that a boy's moral training depended in
large degree upon the character of his pedagogue, and
that, as this was not always of the highest, many suffered in consequence.

It is not easy to determine how the daily programme
of an Athenian school was arranged; but it is not un-
likely that the younger boys went to the palæstra in

6

the morning and to the music-school in the afternoon, while the older boys did the reverse. Assuming this, we shall follow the younger boys through a day. Arrived at the palæstra, they salute the training-master, pay their respects to Hermes, the patron deity of physical culture, whose statue and altar occupy a prominent place, and then begin their exercises. These are suited to the age of the boys, and are therefore neither violent nor complicated. Their aim is to develop all the faculties of the body in a harmonious way, and to make it the ready and effective instrument of the will. No attempt is made to impart the athletic habit. The exercises consist of (1) running, (2) leaping, (3) discus-throwing, (4) javelin-casting, (5) wrestling. The first two are meant to exercise the legs, the second two the arms and eye, the last the whole body and the temper. These exercises are varied with lessons in dancing and deportment, whose purpose is to impart ease, grace, and dignity to every attitude and movement, and to do away with awkwardness, forwardness, and bashfulness. A good deal of time also is given up to play, during which the boys are allowed considerable freedom, and enjoy excellent opportunities for learning the principles of concerted action and of justice. In this way the forenoon is spent. About noon there is a recess, during which the boys partake of a simple meal brought them by their pedagogues.* After this the boys are marched

---

* I am inclined to think that this was the custom in the olden time, although, so far as I know, there is no express statement in any ancient author on the subject. At a later time, if we may judge from certain implied reproaches in Xenophon's *Education of Cyrus*, the boys went home to lunch, and often received im-

in order to the music-school. Here, after saluting the master, and uttering a beief invocation to the Muses and Apollo, whose statues adorn the schoolroom, they begin their mental gymnastics. These consist of singing, playing on the lute (κίθαρις), writing, and reading. The boys sit on the ground or on low benches, while the teacher, armed with a rod, occupies an elevated seat. The exercises open with patriotic songs. The first is a religious song celebrating Zeus, Athena, or some great deity, and is sung in unison to a simple, old-fashioned Doric air; and the boys are encouraged to throw all the fire they can into both words and music. This is followed by a war-song recalling some great national victory, and is rendered in the same spirit. Then follow other songs of different kinds, but all simple and strong, appealing to patriotic and ethical emotions quite as much as to the musical sense. After the singing comes the lesson on the lute, in which the boys learn to play the airs to which their songs are sung. After the lute-playing comes the instruction in letters (γράμματα). Each boy holds in his hands a wax-covered tablet, or rather a pair of folding tablets, and a stylus. These tablets contain the writing lesson of yesterday, which is the reading lesson of to-day. The boys go up in turn to the master, who punctuates the writing for them—that is, separates words and clauses (διαστίζει) *—and then the

---

proper food from overindulgent mothers. It does not seem that at any time the training-master exercised any supervision over the eating and drinking of his pupils, this being probably left to the parents and pedagogues. At this time the Greeks were a temperate people, so that no special training in dietetic hygiene was necessary.

* I am supposing that the boys we are following have already

reading begins. The first effort of the master is to make the boys read without stumbling or hesitancy (ἀδιαπτώτως) ; having accomplished this, he proceeds to make them read with due regard to expression, prosody, and pauses (καθ' ὑπόκρισιν, κατὰ προσῳδίαν, κατὰ διαστολήν), and only after this has been done to his satisfaction does the reading-lesson close, when the boys are reminded that they are expected to commit the whole to memory against exhibition-day. Other tablets are now produced, and the writing-lesson begins. This is at the same time a dictation-lesson, for the boys write down what the master recites. With this the session closes, the rest of the day till sunset being devoted to play under the eye of the pedagogues, who at last see their wards safely home before the streets are dark.

It is not pretended that the above picture is correct in every particular ; but, on the whole, I believe it fairly represents the daily life of an Athenian school-boy between the ages of seven and eleven. The above programme may seem to us rather meagre. There is no arithmetic, no grammar, no geography, no drawing, no physical science, no manual training — only physical exercise, dancing, singing, playing, reading, and writing. And yet, if we examine the programme carefully, we shall see that it was admirably adapted to the end in view, which was to make strong, well-balanced, worthy, patriotic citizens, capable, through bodily strength, courage, social motive, and intelligence, of meeting every emergency of civil and military life.

---

learned to write all the letters and syllables. This they usually did on boxes of sand or on sand strewed on the ground. The tablets were used when dictation began.

The first thing that strikes one about it is that it aims at developing capacity and not at imparting accomplishments or knowledge. Its purpose is to put the pupil in complete possession of his bodily and mental powers, so that he may be ready to exert them wisely in relation to anything that may present itself. Such self-possession was called by the Greeks καλοκάγαθία, fair-and-goodness, the "fair" applying to the body, and the "good" to the soul. Again, if we look at the intellectual part of the programme, we shall find that it is not so meagre after all. The poetry which forms the matter of it holds in solution a whole world of valuable experience and moral example, which it only requires a good instructor to bring out. The poetry of Greece was its religious and ethical lore; Homer and Hesiod were its Bible. In learning this poetry, therefore, boys were imbibing the very essence of the national life, the inner spirit, of which its history and institutions were but the external embodiment. There are two things which the Greeks recognized far better than we do : (1) the educational value of true poetry, and (2) the ethical influence of works which present in artistic form the principles, religious and political, of a people's life. We are inclined to be content if we can get information rapidly and easily into the heads of our pupils, and trouble ourselves very little about the manner in which this is accomplished. The Greeks were wiser. They knew that the how is more important than the what; that conceptions which are presented to the mind clothed in poetic light and heat are far more readily assimilated and retained, and exercise a far deeper and more lasting influence upon the imagination, the feelings, and the will, than those which come to it in the cold, gray garb of ordinary prose. They knew that to accustom the mind to a poetic way of conceiving things, and of expressing its conceptions in the forms of language, is far better than to crowd it with any number of facts, however useful. The truth is, the world at bottom is poetical, and unless we can see it poetically we do not see it as it is.

Again we are inclined to think that any piece of writing is good enough to put in a reading-book for schools, provided it is free from grammatical errors and interesting or amusing. "The One-horse Shay" or "The Owl and the Pussy-cat" does just as well as "The Landing of the Pilgrim Fathers." In this again the Greeks were wiser than we. From the time when their sons began to read, the great literary works of the nation were placed in their hands, and the thoughts and ideals which had shaped the institutions of the state made familiar to their thoughts and imaginations. Such was the richness of these works that there is hardly any branch of ordinary education recognized at the present day that might not easily be brought into fruitful and elevating connection with them.* And there can be no doubt that in the hands of good teachers they were made the basis not only of ethical instruction, but also of history, geography, grammar, and many other things.

If now we should follow one of the older boys through his exercises for a day, we should not find that they differed greatly from those of the younger

---

* Greek literature was admirably adapted for educational purposes; but English is not one whit behind it. What a glorious day for English and American education it will be when the school-books are the Bible, Shakespeare, Scott, and Tennyson!

boys, except in being more advanced and in demanding more continuous and vigorous exertion. The
races, the leaps, the throws of discus and javelin, become longer; wrestling becomes more complicated
and energetic, and occupies more time than formerly.
Preparation is going on to meet the dangers of the
approaching age of puberty. The poetry and music
are of a higher order; the literary lessons are longer,
treat of higher and more abstruse subjects, and are
made the basis for more difficult studies. Arithmetic
is now introduced, and some elementary instruction
given in astronomy. When the age of puberty arrives,
a marked change is made in the studies. More time
than before is devoted to physical training, while the
intellectual exercises assume a more practical turn.
Every effort is made to fill the time of the boys with
vigorously active occupations, to turn their attention
outward, away from themselves and their own feelings
and toward things to be done. Emulation, which always played a principal part in everything Greek, is
now allowed to have its full effect, and superiority in
any study rewarded with all that is dear to the heart
of a boy. And this leads us to the matter of school
exhibitions.

We have already seen that physical training was
under the patronage of Hermes, while music and letters were under that of Apollo and the Muses. Now,
since such patronage always implied worship, certain
days were set apart in all the schools for this purpose.
The palæstras celebrated the Hermæa ('Ερμαια); the
music schools, the Musea (Μουσεῖα). At these festivals
the religious service consisted of competitive exercises
on the part of the pupils, closing with a sacrifice. By

a law of Solon's the school buildings and grounds were at these times, as at all others, rigorously closed against grown persons, and any one who entered was liable to the penalty of death. Thus the only spectators, besides the teachers and their families, were the impartial gods. Before the sacrifice the successful competitors were crowned with wreaths, and were the heroes of the occasion, being regarded as the special favorites of the patron gods, whom they had proved themselves to have worthily served; for all worth or excellence was regarded as a mark of divine favor, and its manifestation a part of divine service.

About the age of sixteen the Athenian boy finished his school life. This was a most important event in his career; for now he passed, in great measure, out of the hands of his parents into those of the state, which undertook to complete his education and prepare him for citizenship. It is a curious fact that, in spite of all the recommendations of philosophers and the example of Sparta, Athens never had any system of public instruction, except what was needed as a direct preparation for civil and military service. Wisely, I can not but think, she refused, by a socialistic system of public schools, to relieve parents from the duty of educating their children, a duty which they had undertaken in bringing them into the world. At the same time, she recognized perfectly well her duty to her children and future citizens by imposing certain disabilities upon parents who failed to educate their sons, and by making inaccessible to uneducated boys the instruction necessary to prepare them for the higher duties of citizenship.

It seems to me probable that state-education for

state-purposes originated with Solon, who did so much for the culture of his fellow-countrymen. It was he who built the first gymnasia at Athens, the Academy to the northwest of the city, and Cynosarges to the east, the former as a resort for full-blooded citizens, the latter for those whose blood contained a foreign admixture. These gymnasia played an important part in the life of the people. They were not only public parks and exercise-grounds where the citizens spent a good deal of their time, but they were also state educational institutions, subserving, in an unobtrusive way the interests of aristocracy. While no young man born of free parents was excluded from them, yet, inasmuch as no one was fitted to enter who had not received a careful previous education in school and palæstra, their benefits were practically confined to the sons of cultured and well-to-do families; and since only those young men who had taken a full state-course of instruction in the gymnasia were eligible to the higher state-offices, the result of the establishment of these institutions was to confine these offices to members of such families. So long, therefore, as the constitution of Solon remained in force, the state-gymnasia formed a barrier against the rising tide of democracy.

When a boy was admitted to a public gymnasium, though still regarded as a minor, he obtained a sudden and often perilous accession of liberty. He was no longer accompanied by his pedagogue when he went abroad, but was free to go where he liked—to lounge in the streets or the agora, to choose his own companions, and to be present at whatever was going on in the city. A good deal of his time was no doubt spent in his gymnasium, in physical exercises, and in pleasant walks and talks with companions of his own age and with older men. The exercises were now what was known as the *pentathlon*, consisting of running, leaping, discus-throwing, wrestling, and boxing. They were superintended by a state-officer (γυμναστής or ἀλείπτης), who saw to it that they were conducted in the most vigorous manner. Before the wrestling-lesson began, the young men were rubbed over with oil and bestrewed with fine sand, and then began a wild struggle, literally in the dirt; for care was taken to teach them that, when occasion demanded, they must not be afraid of soiling their hands or even their whole bodies.* When the lesson was over they scraped themselves with a strigil, took a cold bath, were again anointed, and then rested, exposing their naked bodies to the sun, till the skin became of a light chestnut color.† The boxing lessons seem to have been conducted in a way not unworthy of the modern prize-ring. It hardly needs to be remarked that all the exercises in the gymnasia were public, a fact which was enough to deter weaker men from taking part in them, and to encourage the stronger ones to do their best.

It is a curious circumstance that during the years

---

* See the graphic account in the beginning of Lucian's *Anacharsis:* "They are mixed up in the dirt, rolling about like pigs" (ἐν τῷ πηλῷ συναναφύρονται, κυλινδούμενοι ὥσπερ σύες), and more to the same effect.

† This curious practice enables us to account for the color on the bodies of certain recently discovered painted statues, and also for the sneers of Aristophanes at the pale complexions (τοὺς ὠχριῶντας, *Clouds*, 104) of the pupils of Socrates.

when young men were attending the public gymnasia
no intellectual instruction, not even a course in political science, was provided for them. The explanation of this clearly is that they were expected to acquire
all that was necessary from attending courts, public
meetings, etc., and from contact, in the gymnasia and
agora, with older men. The truth is that in Athens
what we should call college-education was imparted
directly by the state through its ordinary functions.
Thus her young men, instead of attending classes in
political science, gave their attention to the practical
application of political principles in the daily life of
the state.

The gymnastic training of the young Athenian
lasted for two years. At the age of eighteen, if he had
worthily acquitted himself, he graduated, taking the
degree of *cadet* (ἔφηβος), and passed out of the control
of his parents into that of the state. This transition
was accompanied with an impressive ceremony. His
father, having proved from the records of his phratry
that he was the lawful child of free parents, had his
name enrolled in the register of his *demos*, and the
youth became a member of it. Thereafter, furnished
with the necessary credentials, he presented himself to
the so-called king-archon (ἄρχων βασιλεύς), and asked
to be introduced to the people as a citizen. He now
cut off the long hair which he had previously worn,
and put on the black dress which marked the citizen.
At the first public meeting held thereafter the archon
introduced him, in company with others, to the whole
people. Hereupon, armed with spear and shield (the
gift of the state, if he was the orphan son of a father
who had fallen in battle), he proceeded to the temple

of Aglauros, which overlooked the agora, the greater
part of the city, and a large portion of the territory of
the state, and here took the following oath, prescribed
by Solon: " I will never disgrace these sacred arms,
nor desert my companion in the ranks. I will fight
for temples and public property, both alone and with
many. I will transmit my fatherland, not only not
less, but greater and better, than it was transmitted to
me. I will obey the magistrates who may at any time
be in power. I will observe both the existing laws and
those which the people may unanimously hereafter
make, and if any person seek to annul the laws or set
them at naught, I will do my best to prevent him, and
will defend them both alone and with many. I will
honor the religion of my fathers. And I call to witness Aglauros, Enyalios, Ares, Zeus, Thallo, Auxo, and
Hegemone."

But though after this the young men were full citizens, they were not permitted to exercise all the functions of such. For two years more they were regarded
as novices, and took no part in civic duties, being compelled to live outside the city, to garrison fortresses,
and to act as patrolmen and country police. Their
life at this time was that of soldiers in war, and
woe to them if they showed any cowardice or weakness! If during the two years they ca. ie up to the
required standard of manhood, and passed the manhood examination (δοκιμασία εἰς ἄνδρας), they received
the degree of Athenian man,* returned to live in the

---

* Public speakers always addressed the citizens by this title
("Ἄνδρες 'Αθηναῖοι, Athenian men), which is quite different from
simple "Athenians" (ὃ 'Αθηναῖοι).

city, and began to exercise all the duties of citizenship. Their university, their *alma mater*—and they attended it for the rest of their lives—was the state; their curriculum, their civic duties. During the earlier years of their civic life their time was pretty fully occupied with practical duties—administrative, judicial, military; but as they approached the age of fifty they enjoyed more leisure, which they devoted to διαγωγή, this being regarded as the crown and just reward of a well-spent life.

Such, in its general outlines, was the scheme of Athenian education in the centuries which preceded the Persian war and the rise of philosophy, and it may be taken as the type of Greek education generally during that time. Those great educational differences which in subsequent times fixed so wide a gulf between Athens on the one hand, and Thebes and Sparta on the other, existed as yet but in embryo. How valuable this scheme was, and how well adapted to its purpose, was shown to all the world on the fields of Marathon and Platææ and in the Gulf of Salamis, when it broke the power of Oriental despotism forever and laid the foundations of human freedom.

CHAPTER IV.

GREEK EDUCATION AFTER THE RISE OF PHILOSOPHY.

THERE is no date in Greek history upon which we can put a finger and say, Here philosophy began. The progress from unreflective to reflective thought was slow and laborious, and the latter did not appear until it was called for by new social relations for which the former was found to be inadequate. Like every other great spiritual product which gave lustre to Greek civilization, philosophy took its first steps, not in Greece proper, but in those of her colonies which came in contact with civilizations different from hers—in Ionia first, and in Magna Græcia afterward—and all the philosophers before Socrates belong to one or the other of these regions. Just what the circumstances were which first made men feel that the old, simple, mythical explanation of the origin and order of the world was unsatisfactory, and forced them to look about for another, we can not tell with certainty; but there are some reasons for concluding that among them was that confusion of myths which arose out of the attempt to unite religions of widely diverse character—attempts which could hardly fail to be made in the regions above referred to. Not seldom does a conflict between rival claims result in the rejection of both, and the putting forward of a new claimant. And so it hap-

pened in this instance. In the conflict of mythologies
—Greek, Lydian, Persian, Phœnician, etc.—mythology
came gradually to be discredited and to be superseded
by philosophy.

We have seen that in the earlier stages of social
existence life rested upon a religious consciousness—
that is, upon a strong, unreasoned feeling of the solidarity of the family, phratry, tribe, etc. We have also
seen that this solidarity originally included the dead
as well as the living members of the social body, and,
being supposed to depend upon community of blood,
gave occasion to sacrificial rites, which were merely a
means of maintaining and strengthening it. We have
seen, still further, that these rites were continued long
after their meaning was forgotten and the worship of
nature-powers had replaced that of ancestors, nay, even
after nature-powers had given way before ideal moral
personalities. With each of these substitutions, of
course, religious rites assumed a new meaning. The
rise of nature-powers gave birth to mythology; that of
moral personalities to ethical allegory and Orphic the-
osophy. But, despite all such changes, the rites persisted, and life continued to rest upon a sense of solidarity between the individual and his social and
physical environment, a sense which is the origin of
all religion. Moreover, in proportion as the true
meaning of religious rites was forgotten, the rites
themselves came to be invested with an atmosphere
of mystery, which gave them a vague and awesome impressiveness, such as no amount of clear meaning could
have imparted to them. It was in this way that religion, which originally had nothing to do with ethics,
came to furnish ethical sanctions, and to be regarded

as something against which it was impious to utter a word. In brief, the sacredness of religious observances and beliefs is in great measure due to their mysteriousness.

Now, as long as there is no conflict of religious observances and of beliefs connected with them, they are found to furnish very strong sanctions for external morality; but let a conflict arise, and their influence is gone, and then other sanctions must be sought for. These new sanctions, generally speaking, can be found only through reflection—that is, philosophy. Such is the origin of Greek philosophy. Of course, the passage from religion to philosophy is gradual, and the latter is long in finding out what its implications are. It was not till Socrates came that Greek philosophy really became conscious of what it meant; and then, naturally enough, religion tried to abolish it in his person.

The aim of what has been said thus far is to bring out the fact that, with the rise and growth of philosophy, life loses its old religious basis and seeks to find another through reflection. But religion, being at bottom a sense of solidarity, which is the fundamental bond of society, when this sense is gone, society is liable to fall to pieces, unless a bond of equal strength can be found in philosophy. And it is long before this can be done. Reflection in its infancy turns to the physical world, to which, indeed, the old gods belong, and there, apart from gods, it finds no moral sanctions—nothing calculated to hold society together. It is only long afterward, when it turns its attention inward to the spiritual world, that it discovers the true bond, which is no longer one of blood or land, but one of intellect and will; and it is only then that men can pass from natural to moral life and religion.

We need not, then, be in the least surprised when we find that the first effect of reflective thought was to loosen the old bonds of society and reduce it to its constituent atoms, or individuals, for *individual* is only the Latin rendering of the Greek *atom* (ἄτομον). In a word, philosophy gave rise to individualism. Nor is this wonderful; for one chief difference between unreflective and reflective thought is this: the former is race-thought, the latter individual thought, and each tends to preserve its own subject and to invest it with importance. The struggle between the two kinds of thought was long and fierce, and did not—indeed, could not—close until men discovered that neither the one nor the other was true by itself, but that the two had to combine in universal or divine thought. We can well sympathize with Heraclitus when, seeing the social ravages of individualism, he exclaims: "Though reason (λόγος) is universal, the mass of men live as if each had a private wisdom of his own!" In the midst of this struggle ancient society, with its material ties, fell to pieces, and the world has been struggling ever since to replace it by a social order bound together by spiritual, that is, ethical, ones.

The same contact with foreign peoples which gave the impulse to reflective thought among the Greeks also brought about that ever-memorable conflict which first made Greece conscious of her own mission, lifted her to a new grade of civilization, and made necessary an ethical social bond. When, after the second Persian war, Athens assumed the hegemony of Greece, and sud-

7

denly found herself compelled to deal with a large number of confederate states, she confronted a problem for
which her political experience and principles had not
prepared her—the problem of how to combine with
her associates into a larger and stronger political unity.
What shall be the bond of this unity? was now the
vital question ; and Athens returned the wrong answer.
Instead of seeking to introduce an ethical bond between herself and her associated commonwealths, to
be merely *prima inter pares*, and so to pave the way
for a United States of Greece, she tried to reduce them
to a condition of material dependence, and in the end
ruined both herself and them. But the principles
which she had refused to apply in order to found a
social order deserving to absorb and supersede her
own, were all the while at work in her own body,
slowly but surely accomplishing its dissolution. Individualism was shaping itself into democracy, which
was entirely incompatible with the existence of the
ancient state. Democracy requires a moral bond, and
the ancient state had only a material one.

The spirit of individualism, fostered by reflective
thought, showed itself nowhere sooner than in education. Aristotle says : " When they (our ancestors) began to enjoy leisure for thought, as the result of easy
circumstances, and to cherish more exalted ideas with
respect to worth, and especially when, in the period
before and after the Persian wars, they came to enter-
tain a high opinion of themselves on account of their
achievements, they pursued all kinds of education,
making no distinction, but beating about generally."
The truth was, to the new thought, not bounded by
the horizon of a small state and its round of duties,

the old education seemed narrow and meagre, and, like any other novice, it grasped at everything that came within its reach, especially in states which, like Athens, had no public system of education. Thus there arose a demand for all kinds of knowledge, for polymathy,* as the Greeks said, without any regard to its value for the practical business of life—for knowledge which, at best, might serve the purposes of διαγωγή, now gradually coming to claim a large share in life. This demand brought into existence a class of men not hitherto known in Greece—men who called themselves Sophists (σοφιστής, one who makes wise) and undertook to teach everything. To some extent they took the place of the old rhapsodes; indeed, they might fitly enough be termed philosophic rhapsodes, inasmuch as they bore the same relation to the philosophers who preceded them as the rhapsodes bore to the epic poets. Since the days of Socrates the name Sophist has had an evil sound, implying shallowness and charlatanry; and this is not altogether unjust to the bearers of it. Nevertheless, the Sophists were the natural product of their time, which was in the main responsible for their characteristics. Their work was mostly negative and destructive, but it had to be done. Their disorganizing influence was due not so much to their self-satisfied foppish agnosticism as to the importance which they assigned to the individual con-

---

* Heraclitus, who evidently despised this, says: "Multitude of knowledge (πολυμαθίη) does not teach understanding, else it would have taught Hesiod and Pythagoras, and again Xenophanes and Hecatæus." The four men here mentioned evidently represent to the Ephesian the new tendency, which he deplores.

sciousness. Their fundamental tenet, "Man (i. e., the individual man) is the measure of all things," expresses the essence of individualism. At the same time, it is only a clear assertion of the validity of reflective thought, as opposed to the unreflective thought of the preceding ages; and it was well that this assertion should be boldly made. For the first time in the world's history rationalism became conscious of itself and demanded a hearing.

For us of the present day it is very difficult to conceive that the identification of moral personality with individuality is a thing of comparatively recent date; that in the earlier ages even of Greece, Rome, and Israel this had not been accomplished. And yet it is true. In those times the moral personality was not the individual, but the social organism, the family or the state, as the case might be. In the old Hebrew commandment God is said to "visit the iniquity of the fathers upon the children unto the third and fourth generation," and it is not till the time of Ezekiel, a contemporary of Solon's, when the Hebrew social organism is in ruins, that we find the announcement: "The son shall not bear the iniquity of the father, neither shall the father bear the iniquity of the son; the righteousness of the righteous shall be upon him, and the wickedness of the wicked shall be upon him." * If among the Hebrews this conviction was the result of social disorganization, among the Greeks the opposite was the case; social disorganization was the result of the conviction that the individual stands for himself alone.

---

* Ezek. xviii, 20. The whole of the chapter ought to be read in this connection.

It is easy enough to understand that such a change of view should revolutionize the whole life of a people. As long as the social organism was the moral personality, so long it was the centre of interest and effort; but no sooner was its place taken by the individual than all interest and effort were transferred to him, and the social organism, if not neglected, was regarded as a means of which individual good was the end. In Greece this momentous change was wrought mainly through the Sophists. From their time Greek education tended more and more to lose sight of the citizen in the man and to regard practical life a mere means to διαγωγή. Let us see what the immediate effect of this was upon the two acknowledged branches of instruction—gymnastics and music.

In the old time, as we have seen, the aim of gymnastics had been to impart vigor and grace to the body, so that the pupil might perform his part as a citizen with energy and dignity, in war and peace. Now it becomes more and more a preparation for cultured leisure, for an easy self-sufficient enjoyment, such as men were beginning to look forward to in Elysium,* but which they tried to anticipate here on earth. There is a passage in Pindar which shows very clearly what this enjoyment in his time was expected to be. "For them below there shines the might of the sun during the night here, and in meadows of purple roses their sub-

---

* The belief in personal immortality, with bliss or bale according to the life here, did not, and could not, become clear until the individual came to be recognized as the moral personality. Up to that time it was immortality for the nation or the family that was coveted. This was notoriously the case among the Hebrews.

urban retreat is laden with dark frankincense and golden fruits. And some delight themselves with horses and gymnastic exercises, some with draughts, and some with lyres, and with them all prosperity luxuriates in full bloom. And through the pleasant place a perfume is shed as they forever mingle all kinds of scented woods with far-gleaming fire upon the altars of the gods." It is obvious enough that gymnastics having in view a life of this sort, a life of æsthetic enjoyment, will be very different from the gymnastics intended to harden men for the duties of civil life. They will no longer aim to make the body capable of the greatest amount of sustained exertion, but to fit it for such activity as shall give delight and impart the delicious sense of physical health. In a word, their aim will be subjective, not objective; it will be feeling, necessarily confined to the individual, not action exerted for the good of a community. It would be difficult to overestimate the momentousness of this change.

Very similar was the change that took place in regard to "music." In the older period the chief purpose of this branch of education had been to stimulate an intelligent patriotism and to develop those mental qualities which should enable men to play their part worthily in all the departments of domestic and civil life. Knowledge for knowledge' sake was hardly dreamed of. Now, on the contrary, though the old aims are by no means forgotten, new aims of an entirely different sort come in, and not only alter the character of the instruction, but call for new sorts of instruction altogether unknown before. The strong old patriotic songs, with their simple Doric airs, played upon the simplest of instruments—songs whose purpose had been to stir the heart with manly emotions, which might be ready for use as motives when strenuous action was demanded—now gradually give way to languid or sentimental songs with complicated ear-tickling rhythms, set to Lydian or Phrygian airs full of trills and graces, and played upon difficult instruments requiring skilful manipulation. Such songs and music were calculated to fill with sweet delight a passive mood, not to stir the soul to deeds of worth. Aristophanes, the inimitably witty and sincere champion of the olden time, says that if then "any one attempted any fooling, or any of those trills, like the difficult inflections à la Phrynis, now in vogue, he received a good thrashing for his pains, as having insulted the Muses," the patrons of the study. But even Aristophanes's wit could not counteract the new tendency. "The cornet, flute, harp, sackbut, psaltery, dulcimer, and all kinds of music" were introduced into the schools,* and boys learned to play on them, not to develop in themselves worth for action, but to obtain pleasure for themselves, or to make a display for the delectation of others. And while this change was going on in the case of music proper, letters, which were still classed along with music, were following a similar course. The old epic poets were by degrees discarded as old-fashioned, and their place

---

* This was literally true; see Aristotle, *Polit.*, viii, 6; 1341a 40 *sqq.*, where are enumerated πηκτίδες, βάρβιτοι, ἑπτάγωνα, τρίγωνα καὶ σαμβῦκαι, with two etc., the first covering those instruments "that tend to the pleasure of those using them"; the second, to those "that require manipulatory science," or, as we should say, scientific manipulation.

was taken by works of a reflective and didactic sort.
Gnomic poetry, as it was called—that is, epigrammatic
poetry of a sententiously moral kind, such as was written by Simonides, Archilochus, Solon, and Theognis—
came greatly into vogue,* and furnished matter for
casuistic and hair-splitting discussions, which, while
they might sharpen the wits and afford opportunities
for brilliant intellectual sword-practice, were not calculated to strengthen the moral nature or awaken an
enthusiasm for manly activity.† Whereas the epic
poetry had turned the thoughts outward to the world
of deeds and drawn the moral distinctions in it, this
gnomic poetry turned the attention inward to the
world of motives, and tried to draw distinctions among
them. The effect of this, of course, was to foster reflection instead of action. And this reflection, once
roused, turned itself to the whole content of the consciousness and to the forms in which it found expression, thus giving birth, in course of time, to the sciences of logic, rhetoric, and grammar, all of which
may be said to owe their origin to the Sophists. All
of them, too, were sooner or later included in the
school programme, which thus became almost as varied
as that of a modern school.

Thus both branches of education gradually lost
sight of their objective and civic aim, which was
worth, and drifted toward a subjective and individual
one, which, when it became fully conscious of itself,
assumed the name of εὐδαιμονία, or happiness. But

---

* See Aristophanes, *Clouds*, 1036 *sqq.*

† In the first book of Plato's *Republic* (331 E *sqq.*) there is
an example of such discussion, having for its text a gnome of
Simonides' who is acknowledged to be a great authority.

the individualistic influence of philosophy,* as popu-
larized by the Sophists, was not confined to the palæstra and the music-school. With these, indeed, the
Sophists had comparatively little to do. Their chief attention was directed to the young men who were attending the public gymnasia, or who, having passed their
manhood examination, were eager to distinguish themselves in public life or to secure the conditions of happiness. For the moral and intellectual culture of these
two classes of young men the state had made no special
provision, trusting that they would acquire whatever of
this sort was necessary or serviceable through daily contact with older men and in the exercise of the duties
of public life. And this trust, on the whole, was well
founded as long as the state remained the chief object
of concern for every citizen; but no sooner did individualism and the desire for pleasant diagogic life
come into competition with the state than a culture
was demanded which it had no means of supplying.
Here the Sophists found their opportunity. The young
men were to be met everywhere—in the streets, the
market-place, the gymnasia, the taverns, the homes,
etc. The Sophist had only to show himself in order
to be surrounded by a knot of them. He had but to
seat himself in an exedra, or lay himself down under a
tree in the gymnasium, and they crowded round to
hear his wisdom—his manifold stores of unfamiliar
knowledge and his brilliant arguments on any theme
proposed to him. He was soon far more popular

* It should not be forgotten that φιλοσοφία (philosophy),
Pythagoras's modest substitute for the older σοφία (wisdom),
originally included all knowledge not possessed by the mass of
mankind. Its technical use is hardly older than Plato.

with them than the most honored and experienced citizen, who could talk to them only about their country's history and their social duties in simple, serious, unadorned speech. He not only professed to teach everything, from household economy up to statesmanship and virtue itself, but he declared himself ready, for a consideration, to show how the individual might successfully assert himself on all occasions, not only as against his fellows, but also as against the state and its laws. Such brilliant professions did not fall upon deaf ears. Young men placed themselves under his tuition, and paid him large sums, to learn the art of successful self-assertion.

When we consider the necessary effect of such teaching upon the social fabric, we can easily understand why the Sophists and their tendencies were held in abhorrence by all conservative and patriotic persons. Nevertheless, it would be unjust to conclude from this that they were evil and insincere men, seeking to bring about social confusion and to profit by it. They may not have been, individually, models of virtue; but certainly they were not mere clever scoundrels. They were the pioneers of a new and higher social order, whose nature they did not comprehend, and for which, therefore, they worked blindly and negatively. But they did not work the less effectively on that account. They called the validity of the old order in question, loosened its bonds, and prepared it for yielding to a new. The old order had merged the man in the citizen and made public sentiment the ethical sanction; the Sophists were, in their crude way, endeavoring to secure a foothold for the man outside of the citizen and to place the moral sanction within his own breast.

Nor must we allow ourselves to be blinded to the true
nature of their enterprise by the very obvious mischief
which it worked at its first inception. It put an end
(let us hope forever) to institutional ethics, and broke
up the order in which they were embodied; but it
paved the way for a higher sort of ethics and a nobler,
because freer, social system. Indeed, it might fairly
be said that all that is best in modern civilization is
contained in germ in the teaching of the despised
Sophists. Their fundamental maxim, " Man is the
measure of all things," may be made to express the
inmost essence of human freedom.

The Sophists might be despised or combated ;
they could not be disregarded. Their views contained
an element of truth which affected even those who
were most opposed to them, and which was never lost.
From their time on, two mutually hostile tendencies
contend for supremacy in Greek education and life :
(1) the old religious, institutional tendency, which
finds in the state the aim and sanction of all individual actions; and (2) the new, philosophical, individualistic tendency, which makes the most desirable
condition of the individual the sum of all good that
can be striven for. Henceforth an unwearied struggle
goes on between the two ideals Worth (ἀρετή) and
Happiness (εὐδαιμονία), between objective good and
subjective good, and defies the deftest efforts at recon-
ciliation. To trace the course of this struggle will be
the chief object of the remaining chapters.

If we wish to see how the new tendency looked to
those whose affections and convictions were bound up
with the old order of things, we must go to the pages
of Aristophanes. Here, of course, we must not look

for fairness; nevertheless, if we discriminatingly tone down the pictures of the hostile caricaturist, we shall, undoubtedly, arrive at something very near the truth. Aristophanes depicts for us the new tendency chiefly in four spheres of manifestation: (1) education, (2) private morality, (3) public morality, (4) religion, and in each tries to bring out, in all its implications, and to hold up to ridicule and scorn the gospel of individualism. We shall consider these in order.

1. In education he finds that the old endeavor after manliness, simplicity, and modesty has given way to an effeminate indulgence which expresses itself in luxury and irreverence. Boys, instead of going to school, as in the good old days, in marching order, with downcast looks, and with the meagrest of clothing, now find their way to it singly, staring impudently at every one they meet and making a show with the heavy clothing in which their pampered limbs are wrapped, and which makes free activity impossible. Arrived at the music-school, instead of striking up some of the old, heroic national songs, and singing with a gusto their simple Doric airs that stirred the blood and warmed the heart, they tune their feeble voices in Lydian measures to some languishing, sentimental love-ditty, which makes them conscious of themselves and their slumbering passions, or in plaintive Phrygian elegiacs to some epigrammatic, moral gnome, which provokes reflection and morbid self-introspection. Passing to the palæstra, they are more eager to display the charms of their smooth and delicate bodies than to harden them by vigorous exercise, more careful to leave an impression of them in the sand, to suggest lewdness, than an impression of the sand upon them. When they return home,

they are bold, irreverent, and disobedient. They sit
with their legs crossed, snatch the daintiest morsels
from the table, gorge themselves with luxuries, talk
back to their parents, call their fathers by the most
disrespectful names, and treat them as insufferable,
old-fashioned bores. When they grow older and are
allowed to go out alone, instead of attending the gymnasia and taking part in their manly exercises with
others of their own age, they lounge about the streets,
squares, and bath-houses, cracking lewd or silly jokes,
or taking part in captious and sophistical disputes
upon matters that have no practical value, perhaps
even flirting with the *demi-monde*. As a result of all
this, they are narrow-chested, sallow-complexioned,
round-shouldered, and—long-tongued. Worse still,
they are utterly corrupt morally, being addicted to
vices of which it is not permitted even to speak.
Such is the sad picture which Aristophanes draws of
the results of individualism on education.

2. Nor is the picture of its effects upon private life
more attractive. Here he finds selfishness, greed, and
dishonesty pervading every relation. Wives are luxurious, shrewish, snobbish, and unfaithful; children are
cunning, self-indulgent, and impure; slaves are lazy,
wasteful, lying, and debauched; husbands, fathers, and
masters neglect their duty to their families and inherited property, and devote themselves to the acquisition
of wealth by low and often dishonest means. Whereas
in the old time families had lived simply and healthily
on the produce of their farms, the possession of which
gave them their title to citizenship, they are now vying
with each other in luxury and display, the means to
which have to be derived from usury or business-profits,

both alike accounted ignoble and unworthy of free
men. Honor has given way to wealth.

3. The effects of individualism upon public life
are summed up for Aristophanes in the one word democracy. Democracy is the horror of horrors, and he
devotes much of his most brilliant and humorous writing to an arraignment of it. He endeavors to show
that, whereas in the old days all political power was in
the hands of the wisest and worthiest men, who used
it for the public welfare, now it is in those of the
basest and most ignorant, who employ it for their
own ends. Instead of the individual's being the devoted servant of the state, as formerly, the state is
now the servant of the individual; politics is a money-
making business. In the sausage-vender (ἀλλαντοπώ-
λης) of the *Knights* he has given us a picture, exaggerated indeed, but vivid and, in its main implications,
true, of the popular politician of his time, with all his
ignorance, stupidity, vulgarity, greed, and bestiality;
and in the same work he has given us another picture,
not less true to life, of the selfish, testy, waspish, pampered, gullible Athenian people, ever ready to put
their faith in any adventurer, however vulgar, who
promises to make life easy and comfortable for the.n,
to give them plenty of anchovies and cushioned seat..

4. But nowhere, according to Aristophanes, has individualism wrought greater evil than in the sphere of
religion. Here it appears as philosophy or reflective
thought, and lays the axe at the very root of the social
tree; for religion, as we have seen, is that root. Aristophanes was entirely right in thinking that the substitution of scientific or philosophic notions for the old
gods must necessarily be fatal to the institutions based

upon the latter. And he finds that they are substituted. Jupiter, Athena, and Apollo have been consigned by the Sophists to the limbo of fable, and in their room have been placed Clouds, Vortex, and—Gab (γλῶσσα)! Even men who are not directly influenced by philosophic ideas have lost faith in the gods, and are either atheists or sunk in gross superstition. In the opening of the *Knights*, Nicias, being asked on what ground he believes in gods, replies: "Because I am an enemy to gods." And further on we are shown what foolish and debasing confidence is placed in fictitious oracles coming from gods and shrines which no one ever before heard of, and which in many cases did not exist.

Thus in every department of social life Aristophanes finds a process of dissolution going on which he foresees must in the end be fatal to the conditions of moral and political life. Accordingly he uses all the resources of his inimitable humor to cast ridicule and discredit upon those whom he conceives to be the chief authors of the mischief—the Sophists. Aristophanes was so far right: the tendency represented by the Sophists did paralyze and ruin the Greek polities; but he was not far-sighted enough to discover that out of that ruin would arise a nobler polity—one not necessarily confined to small communities, but capable of infinite extension, because based on what is purely essential in man. The limitations of his view could not have been shown more strikingly than by his choice of Socrates as the representative of the Sophists. As the reasons for this have rarely been understood, and Aristophanes has been blamed for gross injustice to the great martyr, it will be well to stop for a moment and consider just how far Socrates might with justice be taken to represent the sophistic tendency. Such consideration will help us to understand the subsequent course of Greek education.

We have seen that the rise of philosophy meant the advent of individual and reflective thought, as distinguished from the social and unreflective thought of previous ages. We have seen, further, that the Sophists had formulated the fundamental principle of this thought in the maxim, "Man is the measure of all things," and that in consequence they had striven to remove the criteria of truth and the grounds of action from external traditions and the institutions embodying them, and to place them within the breast of each individual human being. It is obvious that such an undertaking logically compelled them to call in question the reality of all institutional beliefs and sanctions, including the gods and all the mythology relating to them, and that this would necessarily lead to the dissolution of institutions—to what the Greeks called anarchy (ἀναρχία, absence of authority). Now the question is, In how far did Socrates agree with all this?

In the dialogues of Plato and elsewhere Socrates figures so largely as the irreconcilable foe of the Sophists as to have led to the belief that he had nothing in common with them, and that he utterly abhorred their principles and tendencies. Yet this is very far indeed from the truth. In every one of the above positions maintained by the Sophists Socrates was at one with them. No one believed more firmly than he that the ultimate test of truth and sanction of right lies within the breast of each individual; and no man was ever more contemptuous of political, social, or even what claimed to be divine, authority, if it did not carry with it the voice of his inner being. Indeed, it was to maintain this position that he lived and died. The difference between the Sophists and Socrates lay not at all in principles, but in the interpretation of them. When they said, "Man is the measure of all things," they interpreted "man" as the individual man, and then there followed for religion and society all the consequences for which history has held them responsible. Socrates, seeing that absurd moral consequences could not follow from a true principle correctly interpreted, and not being able to fight the Sophists' principle, turned his arms against their interpretation of it, maintaining that the "man" who is the measure of all things is not at all the individual man who eats, drinks, and sleeps, but the transcendent and universal man. What astonishing results for thought and action were the results of this contention we shall see in the next chapter. At present it is enough to say that these results, widely different as they were from those reached by the Sophists, were no less incompatible than those with the religious principles upon which Greek polity rested, however conducive they might be to a polity of a higher order. As far, then, as Aristophanes or any conservative Greek was concerned, there was no difference between Socrates and the Sophists; the principles of both were equally fatal to the old Greek social and moral order. Add to this the fact that the term "Sophist" in Aristophanes's time had none of that special and unpleasant connotation which it afterward acquired, and that in reality Socrates was as much a Sophist as Protagoras; add also the other fact that, while all the other Sophists were foreigners, and therefore comparatively uninteresting, if not unfamiliar, to the body of the Athenian people, and we can have no difficulty in acquitting the great satirist of any unfairness to the yet greater martyr in making him the representative of the disorganizing tendency of rationalism.

It may be supposed from what has been said thus far that the first person to oppose this influence was Socrates, and if we confine our attention to Athens this is true; but just as the effects of philosophy were felt in Ionia and Magna Græcia, where it had its origin, before they were felt in Greece proper, so the efforts to counteract them were first made in those regions. Among the men who put forth such efforts, the most prominent and successful was Pythagoras, of whose attempt to incorporate philosophy with social life we must now take account.

Pythagoras, a native of Samos, was born fully a century before Socrates. It seems that he made his first effort to establish a society on a philosophic basis in his native island, but, being unsuccessful among its Ionians, he emigrated to Magna Græcia, hoping, perhaps, to find more favorable circumstances and a more tractable people among the Achæans and Dorians of that region. Nor was he mistaken. Settling in Croton, and discarding the name "sophist," as too ambitious, for the more modest one of "philosopher," he gathered round him a carefully selected knot of young men, and sought to form them into a society by strict discipline and instruction. His aim was to counteract the disorganizing effects of individualistic reflection, not by any change in the laws or government of the state, but by the formation of a

new organization based upon new principles, outside
of it. He seems to have regarded as useless any attempt to put new wine into old skins, and to have felt
that the new thought demanded a new polity. In considering how such a polity might be called into existence, he saw that the first step was to subject men to
a new system of education involving new principles of
social union. Such a system he then thought out and
applied. It contained three distinct though insepara-
ble elements—(1) a theory, (2) a discipline, (3) a sanction. Though the origin of the first is involved in
obscurity, its gist is not difficult to state. The central
conception of all Pythagoras' thinking is that of Harmony. To him the whole system of the universe is a
harmony, capable of being expressed in terms of number.* As a consequence, all evil, whether in the individual or in society, is nothing but disharmony, and
will disappear when that is removed. To remove it,
and to make man and society follow the same divine
laws that work so unerringly in the starry heavens and
in the whole of Nature, is the aim of all Pythagoras' efforts.† But inasmuch as harmony implies the existence of higher and lower tones standing in a certain
definite relation to each other, Pythagoras, in regard-

---

* Pythagoras is said to have been the first person who used
"cosmos" (κόσμος = order) to designate the world, and I strongly
suspect that the use of ρυθμίζειν (to rhythmicize) in the sense of
"to train" is likewise due to him. It is employed in this sense
by Æschylus and Plato, both of whom show so many other
marks of Pythagoras' influence.

† It is difficult not to believe that the sublime contrast between the order of Nature and the disorder in man, drawn by
the Watchman in the prologue of Æschylus's *Agamemnon*, was
suggested by the teaching of Pythagoras.

ing man and society as harmonies, necessarily endowed them with a series of powers forming an ordered hierarchy. In the case of the individual, highest in the scale came reason, situated in the head; next, life and sensation, located in the heart; next, the nutritive powers, claiming the abdomen; and last, the reproductive powers. How the members of the social hierarchy were named we do not know; but there can hardly be any doubt that they corresponded to those composing the individual hierarchy. Pythagoras' efforts at moral and social reform naturally shaped themselves into an endeavor to give full validity to this hierarchy, so that each higher faculty should govern all below it. Asking himself how this was to be achieved, he answered : " By discipline, through strict obedience to one in whom this hierarchy has been realized," as he believed it had in himself. He accordingly undertook, by a system of strict rules having at first no other authority than his own dictum, to harmonize his pupils, and out of pupils, in the various stages of this process, to form a harmonious social order. In the individual the reproductive powers were to be held in subordination to the nutritive by gymnastics, including careful dieting ; the nutritive, to the sensuous by music ; and the sensuous, to the rational by mathematics, which with Pythagoras occupied the whole sphere of metaphysics. Gymnastics, music, mathematics, these were the three grades of his educational curriculum. By the first the pupil was strengthened ; by the second, purified ; by the third, perfected and made ready for the society of the gods.* There need be little doubt

---

* All this comes out in the clearest way in the famous *Golden Words* (of which see a translation in my *Aristotle*, pp. 57 *sqq.*).

that his pupils were divided into four grades, corresponding to the four elements (τετρακτύς) of the soul-
harmony, each higher exercising authority, direct or
indirect, over all below it, and that this was his type
of the perfect social order.   The supreme authority he
held in his own hands while he lived, and αὐτὸς ἔφα
(HE said so) decided all questions without appeal.
But although this was true, Pythagoras never pretended that his own will furnished the only sanction
for what he did and commanded.   On the contrary,
he claimed to have derived it from the gods, whose
will he conceived to be the harmony of the world.
"Worth and health and all good and God are a harmony," he said.   We need not wonder, therefore, that
he laid great stress upon the worship of the gods and
heroes, with due regard to their rank, and that he
gave much attention to divination, which he tried to
cultivate as a science.

Such, in brief outline, is the educational system of
Pythagoras—a system which aims at universal harmony,
to be realized through discipline, guided by the sanction of divine revelation.   How powerful and enduring its effect upon later theories was, we shall see in
subsequent chapters.   Here it is enough to see that it
is the prototype of all those systems which assume human well-being to depend upon a social order in which
every individual has his appointed place, just as the
system of the Sophists is the prototype of those which
hold that the social order must have its origin in the
wills of the individuals composing it and be the re-
sultant of them.   The former found its highest ex-

Why Zeller should call this work "colorless and desultory"
(*Philos. der Griechen*, vol. i, p. 250) I can not understand.

pression in the Church and Empire of the Middle
Age; the latter is seeking to make itself valid in the
democracies of the modern world.*

---

* The Church was the organ of ascetic or individual discipline; the state, of social discipline; and in true Pythagorean
fashion, the former claimed precedence over the latter, as being
the medium of divine inspiration. It is supremely interesting
to see that our modern Pythagoreans, the Socialists, do not suspect that their fancied Utopias are utterly incompatible with
democracy.

CHAPTER V.

THE EFFORT TO FIND IN INDIVIDUALISM A BASIS OF SOCIAL ORDER.

Up to the date of the struggle with Persia, Sparta had been the leading power in Greece. This was due, in great measure, to the fact that in her, better than elsewhere, was realized the ideal of the city-state. Through the rigorous discipline of her public system of education, which began at birth and ended at death, she forced her citizens to devote themselves, body and soul, solely to her interests and the maintenance of her strength. It mattered nothing to her that this was achieved only through the renunciation of all higher culture. Her ambition was to be strong, and she was so. In this she resembled republican Rome, whose strength was in great measure due to the sedulous exclusion of philosophy, art, and literature. And there can hardly be any doubt that if the city-state had continued to be the supreme object of individual interest, Sparta would have remained at the head of Greece. Her ideal for the individual was worth, and she strove after it with all her might. But in another portion of Greece a new ideal had arisen alongside the old, namely, εὐδαιμονία, or individual happiness. This, though in many respects inferior to the other, had,

like all ideals when they are new, called out in its followers a very large amount of enthusiastic activity. It
had inspired the Athenians with new life; and since it
had not yet weakened their old social bonds, it made
them capable of deeds at which the world still stands
in amazement. It seems to be a fact that the greatest
achievements in the world's history have always been
performed by peoples who were under the inspiration
of a new ideal, but had not lost the social solidarity
due to that which preceded it—a fact which enables us
to understand why brilliant periods are of such short
duration. Certainly this was the case with Athens.
So it came to pass that, when the Persian wars were
over, she found herself, as the acknowledged savior of
Greece, in the position which Sparta had previously
occupied. And she was very proud to occupy it, feeling, as she did, that her powers were adequate to any
task. She was not aware that that exquisite balance
between the old and new ideals, which had made possible her victories in the field and on the sea, could
not long be maintained, and that the new ideal, with
its disorganizing influence, would inevitably soon gain
the upper hand. But such was the case. No sooner
was the enthusiasm of victory over, and the people
were beginning to settle down to the ordinary duties
of social and political life, than the effects of individualism and eudæmonism began to show themselves in
that corruption of all departments of life which, as we
saw in last chapter, called forth the scorn and reproba-
tion of Aristophanes. And Aristophanes was not the
only serious patriot whose anxieties were aroused by
this corruption, or who did his best to put an end to it.
Different persons proposed different remedies. Aris-

tophanes thought to find one in a return to the old order of things, such as had existed before the invasion of reflective thought. Æschylus would probably have recommended the introduction of Pythagorean ideas and discipline. Pericles tried the effect of diverting the people's attention from private social and political complications by the erection of great public works, and subsequently by scheming to form a Greek empire with Athens as its head. But probably not one of these men saw the true source of the corruption and weakness which they all lamented and for which they were seeking to prescribe. This insight was reserved for Socrates, who, though he was not enabled thereby to save his country from ruin, was permitted to discover the principle by which a social order of a far higher type and more inclusive reach was rendered possible for the whole world. Thanks, in great measure, to him, when Greece fell, free humanity rose on her ruins. When she melted away, her life passed into the life of mankind and became its light. Our next task, then, is to consider the origin and nature of the Socratic principle, and then to trace its effects upon Greek education.

In the second half of the fifth century B. C., when Socrates was pursuing his vocation, there were two opposite tendencies at work in the Hellenic world, both of them equally hostile to the existing polities. One, the tendency toward undisciplined individualism, found expression in the teaching of the Sophists; the other, the tendency toward disciplined socialism, in that of Pythagoras. The former was plainly paralyzing and breaking up the social organism; the latter had provoked the most violent opposition and persecution in the regions where it had started, and where, if anywhere, it might have expected to succeed. The Pythagorean communities in Magna Græcia had been broken up with fire and sword and their surviving members scattered throughout the Hellenic world. To Socrates, who with earnest eye was watching the movements of his time, it one day became evident that neither of these tendencies, left to itself, could lead to anything but ruin. He concluded that they must both be wrong in principle; and then there was forced upon him the question, What must be the principle of a movement that will result in social regeneration? Thenceforward the search for this principle was his life-task. He began it by submitting to careful scrutiny the principles of the two tendencies then at work, and as that of the Sophists was affecting his immediate surroundings far more than the other, he directed his first and chief attention to it. "Man is the measure of all things," Protagoras had said. "Yes," mused Socrates, "that is clearly so; for whatever other measure he may apply, must in the last resort be approved—that is, measured—by him. But then, what is man? Who am I?" Socrates was probably the first person in the world that ever addressed that question to himself, and the more he thought of it, the more he was puzzled and staggered by it. He remembered that the Delphic oracle had commanded KNOW THYSELF (γνῶθι σεαυτόν), and he plainly did not know himself. He concluded that, if he did not know himself, he did not know anything, and accordingly made this confession openly. What he meant was that of the knowledge needed to solve the problem before him he had not any; that what people usually called knowledge, that of which the individual man was the measure, was not knowledge at all, but mere opinion (δόξα). He now saw at once that all the evils of individualism came from the attempt to make this opinion the guide and norm of action, and that, before any other guide could be found, some new kind of truth, different from opinion, and not depending, like taste and smell, upon individual idiosyncrasies, must be discovered. This opened up the whole question of the nature of truth and of the human mind as its organ. Up to this time the attention of wise men had been directed to the external world, and what conceptions they had been able to form of it they had naïvely adopted as true without scrutiny and without inquiring whether they were correctly formed. In this way they arrived at opinion, not truth. Socrates now turned his attention inward, and began to ask, What are the conditions for the formation of true conceptions? and, What must be the nature of the being that possesses these conditions? or, again, Who am I?

These are the two most fundamental questions that the human being can ask, and philosophy has no other task than to answer them. It is needless to say that Socrates did not succeed in answering them. At the same time he took the first important steps in that direction. He began by making clear to himself (1) that truth, to deserve the name, must be true for everybody and not depend upon individual peculiarities; (2) that this is possible only if all intelligences, as such, are in some way one intelligence, or have a necessary common content. He saw that, if he could establish the truth of these postulates, he might fairly conclude that the measure of all things is not the individual, as such, but the individual in so far as he shares in the common intelligence, which is the true subject of all truth.* As the question was one which, from its very nature, could not be decided by the individual intelligence, he went about the world examining his fellow men to see whether they had a common intelligence, and, if so, to discover what the content of that intelligence was. "That content," he said, "will be truth and the true social bond." In pursuing this examination, which he did through conversation, he developed his famous method, subsequently called the dialectic, that is, conversational, method. This consisted in taking any conception as it lay in the individual mind and, by a process of induction, showing its limitations and self-contradictoriness; then, by removing these limitations and bringing the conception out with all its relations and implications, proving that it was the same for all intelligences. The conclusion which he himself drew, and which he wished his interlocutors and hearers to draw, was that men think differently only because they think imperfectly, superficially, one-sidedly, and do not see the full meaning of their own thoughts. Complete thoughts are the same for everybody. Having satisfied himself upon this point, he next endeavored to make a list of such complete thoughts as bore more directly upon moral life—courage, temperance, worth, friendship, etc.—and to show their interconnection, so that, presenting themselves as an ordered system of universal truth,

---

* It is easy to see how such a conclusion as this opened the way for the pantheism of the Neoplatonists, the "one intelligence" of the Arabs, and the panlogism of Hegel.

they might be made the basis of a new social order and the material of a new education. It does not seem that he ever advanced so far as to formulate to himself all that is implied in the existence of universal truth; but he did see that, in order to be the subject of it, man must contain something more than his individuality, something more than Protagoras had found in him, and that without it no public morality and no social order were possible. He drew only the ethical conclusions, leaving the ontological for others to draw. Moreover, it does not seem that he was ever able to put his conclusions into a practical form, or to suggest any method by which they might be embodied in actual social life; but he certainly would have deprecated the disciplined socialism of Pythagoras as much as the unbridled anarchism of the Sophists. If the latter left men a congeries of atoms, held together by no force at all, the former bound them into an iron system by an external force, depriving them of that autonomy which is the very condition of moral life, and which it was Socrates' special mission to bring to light and to champion.

The dialectic method played a great part in all subsequent education, philosophy, and religion, nay, even in politics, and its effects were partly good and partly evil. As a means of refuting the sophistic position, and demonstrating the presence of a universal element in human reason, it was invaluable. If it did not enable Socrates to find out what he was, it showed him at least what he was not—viz., a creature of sense with only a subjective consciousness, as Protagoras had held. Again, as a means of revealing the laws of thought and exposing the fallacies of sophistic reasoning, it did admirable service, paving the way for the science of logic. But when it was assumed to take the place of experience and to reveal the content of thought as well as its form or laws, when it was supposed to enable men to ascend to a vision of the eternal powers or realities of which the phenomenal world offers but a faint and passing reflection, then it did infinite harm. It led those who incautiously employed it, not only to distinguish subjective sense from objective intelligence, which was well, but to separate the two and regard them as belonging to two different worlds—one wholly evil and the other wholly good, one from which, and the other to which, it was man's duty to escape. This unjustified separation, with its evil results to education, philosophy, and religion, has haunted the world from Socrates' day to our own. In education it has encouraged asceticism and withdrawal from the world; in philosophy, intellectualism and formal idealism; in religion, inactive contemplation and dread of the senses. In all departments it has led man to mutilate his nature, and to strive to throw away one part as worthless, instead of doing his best to sanctify it as a whole.

These different effects of the dialectic method were not slow in manifesting themselves even in the lifetime of Socrates. Through his plain but attractive personality, his keen intellect, his quaint humor, his genial irony, his imperturbable temper, his modesty, his professed ignorance, his earnestness, his easy victories over his opponents in dispute, and his affection for young men, he soon became far more popular than the best of the foreign Sophists, with their vanity, pretension, and impatience of contradiction. While

they might leave their hearers full of admiration for
their brilliant speeches and specious arguments, he left
them ashamed of themselves and with a desire to be
better than they were. While they appealed to their
selfish instincts, he woke in them a higher consciousness. While they flattered them, he educated them.
But if Socrates found it necessary to oppose the teaching of the Sophists, which was breaking down the social
and political organization about him, he could not rec-
ommend the naïve popular conceptions which were the
life of that organization. He saw that it was just because these conceptions were feeble and superannuated
that they yielded so easily to the attacks of the Sophists.
Thus, while he was willing to die rather than transgress
the laws of the state, he could not give his countenance
to the popular notions on which the state rested. Thus
it came to pass that, while the whole tendency of his
teaching was constructive, and not destructive, like
that of the Sophists, it was hardly less fatal than
theirs to the existing institutions. Theirs discredited
the sanctions which gave these institutions their authority without offering substitutes; he offered substitutes. Aristophanes' picture of Socrates misrepre-
sents the matter, not the tendency, of his teaching. If
this did save many of the young men of Athens from
the disorganizing poison of the Sophists, it at the same
time turned them away from the external, imaginary
deities of their country, and encouraged them to look
for another deity in the depths of their own consciousness. And however far, in a spirit of conciliation or
compromise, he might try to interpret the new sanctions in terms of the old (as many men did before and
have done since), he could not transfer the constrain-

ing power of the former to the latter. He might call the moral lawgiver lodged in his own bosom Zeus or Athena, but he could not make any one identify *that* Zeus with the marble statue that stood in the Olympieum, or *that* Athena with the chryselephantine colossus that occupied the Parthenon. And the mere fact that he encouraged his hearers to look into themselves and study their own minds made his influence one which turned them away from prompt and spontaneous political activity, and gave them a bent toward quiet contemplation, which soon came to be placed at the head of the occupations suitable for διαγωγή. Thus it was that Socrates became, as the capital charge against him set forth, an introducer of new gods and a corrupter of youth.

If we ask ourselves what is the difference between the education which existed before the rise of reflective thought and that which Socrates would have recommended, the answer is that, while the former was essentially a preparation for a state and an order of things already existing, the latter was a preparation for a commonwealth that had not yet appeared; the former had a real, the latter an ideal aim; the former was conservative, the latter revolutionary and progressive. It is easy to see that, if the principles of Socrates had been allowed to prevail in education, they would have speedily abolished those limitations, domestic, phratrial, and political, which made the Greek commonwealth possible.

That the teaching of Socrates soon affected the practice not only of the gymnasia, but also of the palæstras and schools, is rendered evident by a passage in the *Lysis* of Plato. Here Socrates is made to relate how, as he was one day walking by the road immediately outside the city-wall, from the Academy to the Lyceum,* he was invited by a knot of young men (νεανίσκοι) to enter an inclosure the door of which stood open. They inform him that they and many other beautiful (καλοί) youths spend their time there. On asking what sort of a club (διατριβή) it is, he is told that it is a palæstra, recently built; but that most of their time is spent in discussions under the direction of a certain Miccus, "a companion and admirer" of his. "Sure enough," says Socrates, "a decent fellow and a capable 'sophist'!" It would seem as if the "palæstra" had been built expressly as a school for the dissemination of Socrates' teaching, and that it was well attended. And one effect of this teaching was that physical training was neglected, and the chief attention given to lectures and discussions (λόγοι), the very thing of which Aristophanes complains so bitterly. That this change in educational practice resulted in a loss of public spirit and a tendency to effeminate self-indulgence is obvious enough from what is related in the dialogue itself. Nor is this to be wondered at when we consider the character of the older Greek education. And here some important reflections suggest themselves.

The old education had depended for its effect upon training and habit, and only to a very small degree upon moral choice. Its purpose was to produce men who should worthily subserve an end which

---

* These were evidently his favorite resorts. They offered the best opportunities for meeting young men beyond school-age. It will be remembered that later on Plato established his school in the former, and Aristotle his in the latter.

they neither set up nor chose—viz., the stability and
well-being of the state. To encourage reflection and
self-initiated action would have been to defeat this
purpose. It need cause no surprise, therefore, that,
when reflection was actually awakened, and could not
again be put to sleep, but persistently obtruded its
rational sanctions, youths, no less than men, who had
never been accustomed to look to it for the motives
of their actions, should have been perplexed, paralyzed,
and demoralized. To this serious risk is always exposed any system of education which tries to substitute habit and training for reflection as the guides
of action. It should always be borne in mind that
habitual action, however serviceable to institutions,
and however necessary as a preparation for moral
action, is not moral action itself. That can be initiated only by reflection, deliberation, and free choice
between understood motives. Strange as it may seem,
the attempt to make persons who have always been
guided by habit act from motives of reflection is almost
certain to result in temporary, if not permanent, de-
moralization of action. That Socrates saw this and did
his best to prevent it among his countrymen is clear
enough; but though he was more than a match for
the Sophists, he had no arguments strong enough to
meet the logic of the moral law.

Sir Henry Sumner Maine, in speaking of the Hellenic origin of progress, says : " Except the blind forces
of Nature, nothing moves in this world which is not
Greek in its origin." * If we consider all forms of
action not due to reflection and choice as springing

---

* *Village Communities and Miscellanies*, p. 238, Amer. edit.

from " blind forces," this is strictly true; but then we must say that the life of the Greeks, as well as of other peoples, before the rise of reflective thought, was guided by these forces. The Greece that originated progress began with Socrates, in whom reflective thought, for the first time in history, became conscious of its own implications. It was in his time, and owing to him, that men first began to lead a moral life, that they passed from the dominion of the laws of nature, use, and wont, and became subject to those of free spiritual reflection. The momentousness of this transition for all departments of human life, only the whole subsequent course of history can reveal.

When Socrates had arrived at the conclusion that the future moral sanction and social bond must be sought in universal intelligence, there still lay before him the problem of how that bond was to be introduced, and made to ingroove itself with that which was then in force. It does not appear that he ever attained to clearness in this matter; but it is probable that he thought the new bond might be gradually substituted for the old without any great wrench or disturbance to the existing order. He had builded better than he knew. He did not see, and very few men have ever seen, that a social bond having its origin in universal intelligence must include every being that participates in that intelligence. Nevertheless, his teaching brought a dim consciousness of this into the Hellenic world, and from that time on, this worked like a leaven, transforming ethnic into cosmopolitan life. Its influence upon education was exactly what might have been expected. Whereas previously the purpose of all instruction had been to produce dutiful citizens, it henceforth more and more aimed at producing self-poised men, thinking for themselves and choosing their own mode of life. More and more those who were subjected to it withdrew from political and practical life, and devoted themselves to philosophic meditation or contemplation, trying to realize in thought and imagination a commonwealth which should be at once a school of virtue and an Elysium of happiness.

If the teaching of Socrates worked disorganizingly in most departments of Greek life—in education, politics, and religion—there was one department in which, as might have been expected, it had a most beneficial and elevating effect. This was art. It is a remarkable fact that the palmy period of Greek art—the period which produced Phidias and Polycletus, Scopas and Praxiteles—coincides exactly with that filled by the activity of Socrates, Plato, and Aristotle. Before this time Greek art had been practiced altogether in the service of the state, and had sought merely to body forth those conceptions which it represented and approved. Its favorite subjects were, of course, gods, heroes, warriors, and victors in gymnastic contests; and in these it was the element of worth, and not that of beauty, that was held to give them importance and a claim to admiration. We have only to look at the pre-Phidian statues in the museums of modern Greece to convince ourselves of the truth of this. They are, for the most part, not lacking in strength and impressiveness; but they are rude, stiff, expressionless, and not seldom grotesque. They are simply the old religious and patriotic melodies done in stone. But from about the time when Socrates' activity as a public teacher begins, a most remarkable change comes over the whole spirit of Greek art.* Not only does the range of subjects widen, but the figures begin to express character. They are no longer dead symbols, but living persons, instinct with purpose and resolution. In a word, they begin to express ideas, to give form and substance to that invisible world which is soon to become the aim of all philosophic thinking and, after a time, of life itself. But the invisible world is conceived as a world of rationality, order, beauty, διαγωγή, and hence the products of art begin to reflect these qualities. Thus art ceases to minister to practical life and becomes master of ceremonies to diagogic life. It no longer seeks to edify, but to satisfy; no longer to rouse to action, but to invite to contemplation. And since this is the true function of art, it was no fault of Socrates' if the influence which his thought exerted upon it made it one of the agents which helped to dissolve the life of the Greeks into that of the great world. All other art—the art of Egypt, Assyria, Persia, the art of Rome and Etruria even—has become a mere element in the history of the past; but Greek art is universal, eternal art, as fresh and beautiful to-day, as capable of satisfying the demands of diagogic life as it was four centuries before our era. Being the expression of eternal reason and truth, it is as enduring as they are.

---

* It should not be forgotten that Socrates himself was originally, as his father had been, a sculptor. Among his works were a Hermes and a group of draped Graces (Πειθώ, 'Αγλαΐα, Θάλεια), which long stood at the entrance to the Athenian Acropolis, and must, therefore, have been of considerable merit.

When Columbus set sail across the untraversed western sea his purpose was to reach by a new path a portion of the old, known world, and he lived and died in the belief that he had done so. He never knew that he had discovered a new world. So it was with Socrates. When he launched his spiritual bark upon the pathless ocean of reflective thought his object was to discover a new way to the old world of little commonwealths and narrow interests, and he probably died thinking that he had succeeded. He did not dream that he had discovered a new world— the world of humanity and universal interests. But so it was; and though mankind are still very far from having made themselves at home in that world, and from having availed themselves of its boundless spiritual treasures, it can never again be withdrawn from their sight, nor the conquest of it cease to be the object of their highest aspirations.

Looking back now over the ground traversed in the last chapter and in this, we can see that between the period of the old political education and the time at which we have arrived there have been three distinct influences at work: (1) that of the Sophists, almost wholly destructive in its immediate effects; (2) that of Pythagoras, almost purely constructive, but employing external sanctions and a rigid ascetic discipline, tending to socialism; (3) that of Socrates, opposed to both these, and endeavoring to maintain the old social order, but upon a new principle derived from reflective intelligence. Each of these influences left its mark upon the school education of Greece. It was through the first that rhetoric and grammar were added to the school curriculum ; musical science, mathematics (arithmetic and geometry), and astronomy * were due to the second; dialectics and drawing, to the third. And so it was that at the beginning of the fourth century B. C. the old simple curriculum of the schools, consisting of singing, a little lute-playing, reading and writing, was widened out into a curriculum which included every one of what were known in mediæval times as the Seven Liberal Arts, with the addition of one more—viz., drawing. While this expansion was progressing in the music-schools, a corresponding contraction was going on in the palæstras. These were, no doubt, still attended; but the physical exercises seem to have become less vigorous and systematic, and the time allotted to them to have been largely occupied with intellectual gymnastics. Thus, as Aristophanes complains, the boys came to have narrow chests and shoulders and large tongues.

But great as was the change that came over the schemes of education in the schools and palæstras, it was not equal to that which took place in the education of young men after they left these institutions, and became, so to speak, pupils of the state. Here the state and the philosopher came into actual competition. While the former claimed the young men for physical and military training, with a view to practical life, the latter claimed them for intellectual training, with a view to diagogic life. And the philosopher generally carried the day, with the result that

---

* It will be remembered that in the school of Socrates, as caricatured by Aristophanes, there stand two new Muses, Astronomy and Geometry. This seems to show that these studies were first introduced into the Athenian schools in the time of Socrates, and perhaps under his influence.

the gymnasia, though not ceasing to be schools for physical training, gradually became schools of philosophy; and it is as such that two of them, the Academy and the Lyceum, have transmitted their names to modern institutions. No doubt many young men still passed the examination for cadetship and went through their two or three years of militia-service; but even during that time they were not safe from the approach of the philosopher, and when it was over and they returned to the city with all the liberties of independent citizens, they were completely in his power. Many of them, accordingly, instead of devoting themselves enthusiastically, as their fathers had done, to the practical business of the state, and trying to attain influence in its councils, turned aside to the more alluring paths of speculative thought. It is difficult for us who can look back upon the long history of speculation, with its few brilliant conquests and many blasted hopes and pitiful failures, to conceive how it looked in those early days, when its unexplored heights seemed to be the very god-inhabited peaks of Olympus, and to be accessible by the easy, if somewhat tortuous, path of dialectics. Beside the world of truth and beauty, which seemed to loom up there, the things of the every-day world looked mean and paltry. Men began to ask themselves why they should toil and struggle, intrigue, dispute, and go to battle for the sake of such poor and transient goods, when in peaceful contemplation the dialectically-trained soul could rise to the possession of all the glory of immortal things. " Philosophy," they admitted, as Novalis did long after, " can bake no bread; but she can procure for us God, Freedom, and Immortality," and what is bread, they asked, in comparison with these? When we fully realize this condition of mind, induced by the new speculative thought, we can easily appreciate the force of that amusing scene in Aristophanes's *Clouds*, in which Socrates appears suspended in a basket and is made to say: "I am walking the air and growing wise about the sun," * with much more of the same sort.

If we now ask ourselves what Socrates really accomplished in the Greece of his own time, and why his influence roused such opposition in conservative circles as to lead to his death, we shall have no difficulty in finding the true answer. He succeeded, in large measure, in counteracting the purely individualistic influence of the Sophists, which was leading to such utter skepticism, worldliness, and materialism in all the departments of life as to threaten the very existence of society; but he substituted for that influence another which, while it led in the very opposite direction, was hardly less fatal to the institutions that then existed. Both influences tended to extremes, and safety and health, as always, lay in the golden mean. Socrates had solved one problem, only to propound two others no less difficult. He had shown that the disorganizing individualistic tendency of sophistic teaching was to be met by the assertion of a principle of social union to be found not in individual opinion, but in universal intelligence; but he had not shown how this principle was to be introduced, while, in asserting it and showing its nature, he had revealed a world which drew men's attention away from the interests of human society al-

---

* Ἀεροβατῶ καὶ περιφρονῶ τὸν ἥλιον, l. 225.

together. Individualism still asserted itself, no longer, indeed, in the form of worldliness, but in that of other-worldliness. There still, therefore, remained the two questions: (1) How shall the new rational principle of social union be introduced? and (2) How shall the ideal world, which rightfully claims man's supreme interest, be brought into harmony with, and made to contribute to the well-being of, the real world of the present? Before we pass to the attempted solution of these problems which we find in the pages of Socrates' successors, we must turn our attention to a most important result of Socrates' activity and method—a result which permanently and deeply affected all future education and morality. I mean the light which was thrown upon the immortality of the individual soul.

No one acquainted with ancient literatures before the advent of Socrates, or at least before the rise of reflective thought, needs to be told how extremely feeble in them all is the consciousness and hope of individual immortality. Whether we look at the poems of Homer or the pre-exilic literature of the Hebrews, the same fact stares us in the face. It is the immortality of the nation, and not that of the individual, that is hoped for and striven after.* If the individual exist at all after he closes his eyes upon this world, it is only as a shadow, a vague, bloodless ghost, in the gloomy depths of Sheol or Hades,† or a

---

* See in Sir W. D. Geddes's edition of Plato's *Phædo* an interesting *excursus* on Phases of Ancient Feeling toward Death.

† Compare the description of Sheol, *Job*, x, 21, 22—"The land of darkness and of the shadow of death; A land of thick dark-

phantom lingering round the scenes of its former life.
A recent writer says of the souls in Sheol that they
"still subsist, though they do not live." * It was only
as men came to turn their attention away from their
bodies and senses, which divide them, and to direct it
upon their intellectual part, by which they are united,
and which plainly neither comes into existence nor
goes out of it with the body, being one with the eternal energy and order of the world, that they begin to
be aware of their own immortality. And this is as it
should be; men could hardly discover their own immortality until they became conscious of that in themselves which is immortal. And this, we may fairly say,
was discovered by Socrates. It is true that he did not
grasp it in all its implications, having confined his attention chiefly to its moral aspects, and hence he never
arrives at a perfectly firm conviction of his own immortality. He feels that the good man *ought to* be immortal, but he does not see how to translate that
"ought to be" into "is." The various arguments for
immortality adduced in the *Phædo* do no more than
establish a strong rational probability. But the principle which he discovered soon came, in other and
better-schooled minds, to exhibit the proof which he

---

ness, as darkness itself; A land of the shadow of death, without
any order, And where the light is as darkness"—with that of
Hades in the eleventh book of the *Odyssey*, and with the cry of
Achilles in the twenty-third book of the *Iliad*, when the ghost
of Patroclus eludes his embrace, "Oh strange! so there is something (τις) in the halls of Hades, a breath and a phantom, but
there is no heart in it at all" (1. 103, 104).

* Dr. A. B. Davidson, *Book of Job* (Cambridge Bible), p. 188,
n. 6. He adds: "'Destruction,' Heb. *abaddon*, is a synonym for
Sheol."

could not find ; and from his time on the firm belief
in individual immortality became, though not universal, nevertheless common in the Greek philosophic
schools, and general among the great mass of the
Greek people. And this belief added to the disorganizing force of philosophic thought.

Indeed, the belief in personal immortality, substituted for the old belief in the immortality of the race
or the nation, gave a new meaning and purpose to the
whole of life, and turned men's activities into new
channels. As long as men felt that their citizenship
was in this world they made all their plans for this
world, and for it alone. " The brief sum of life," says
Horace, " forbids us to begin long hope. Soon the
night will be upon thee, and the ghosts of story, and
the cheerless house of Pluto " (*Odes*, I, 4). But no
sooner did they come to think that their citizenship
(πολίτευμα) was in heaven, as St. Paul says, than they
began to lay their plans for eternity, and to treat their
earthly life as a mere transient preparation for that.
" We ought not," says Aristotle, " to side with those
who counsel us, as being men, to confine our thoughts
to human things, and as being mortals, to mortal
things, but, as far as may be, to play the immortal
(ἀθανατίζειν), and to do our best to live according to
the noblest that is in us." * Men regarded the family,
the state, and all social institutions no longer as ends
but as means, and as valuable only as preparing the
way for a higher life. More than this, instead of conceiving the sanctions of moral life to be derived from
the social bond, as men had formerly done, they now

---

* *Nic. Eth.*, K. 7; 1177b, 31 *sqq.*

held that that bond itself was derived from a moral sanction, originating in a higher order of being, and revealing itself in the individual intellect. Hence the moral solidarity of the individual was no longer with his fellows in family and state, but with the supreme intelligence, whereof family and state were only instruments. Family and state, it was said, were made for man, and not man for them. Man is not the slave, but the lord, of institutions.

It is almost impossible to conceive a greater or more pervasive change in ethical thought and life-purpose than this. Had it come suddenly, it would certainly have rent the social institutions of Greece to pieces like a thunderbolt. Fortunately, it came slowly, and dissolved them almost imperceptibly into the larger life which was preparing to embody the new moral sanctions. In no department of life did the change show itself earlier or more fully than in that of the higher education and its relation to diagogic life. As long as the proper occupations of that life were supposed to be those enumerated by Pindar —riding, gymnastics, draughts, and music—it could hardly claim a great amount of serious consideration, however much it might be coveted; but when for these were substituted dialectics and the contemplation of the eternal world revealed by them, it assumed a very different position and claimed a larger share of time and attention. Indeed, from this time on diagogic life gradually encroached upon practical life and took precedence of it; and, as a natural consequence, education for the former, in the same degree, took precedence of education for the latter.

In following the steps of this change, we should be

following the process whereby the Greek man disen-
tangled himself from the Greek citizen and laid claim
to a world in which the citizen had no part. In doing
this he set an example for all the world, and began a
new era in human history—the era of moral freedom.
I have treated this change and its causes with some
detail and emphasis, because I think that certain educational and social phenomena of our own time show
that its meaning has not even now been generally apprehended with any clearness, that we do not yet know
how to take full advantage of the victory which the
Greeks won for us. In education we are still trying
to obtain socially desirable results by means of habit,
surroundings, and institutional sanctions, instead of
directly appealing, through the intelligence, to the
moral nature and rousing in it the consciousness of
universality—or autonomy, which is at bottom the
same thing. In social life we are allowing economic
complications to make us look with a half-favorable
eye upon schemes which would, if realized, go far to
identify again the man with the citizen, and to de-
prive him of his moral liberty, through which alone
he is man, for the sake of physical comfort, the enjoyment of which does not differentiate him from the pig
—to use the plain word of Socrates. We are not keeping with sufficient steadiness before our eyes the fact,
revealed so clearly by the history of Greek education,
that the possibility of continuous progress in civilization depends upon our not sacrificing the freedom of
the individual to any ideal static institution which
may promise a certain more or less uniform modi-
cum of well-being for all. We are forgetting that the
ultimate good of man consists not in what he has, but

in what he is, and that he can be nothing at all except through the exercise of moral freedom, which may celebrate some of its noblest victories through that very struggle which our present tendencies are trying to eliminate from life.

CHAPTER VI.

THE ENDEAVOR TO FOUND AN EDUCATIONAL STATE ON PHILOSOPHICAL PRINCIPLES, AND ITS RESULTS.

SOCRATES had sought to show that the true bond of social life must be looked for in the content of that intelligence by which, through their very nature, men are united. He had broken completely with the old blood- and land-bonds, and, though he retained the worth bond, he gave it a new significance by making it depend upon knowledge. It remained to give objective reality to the new combining principle by making it the basis of a new social order.

Though it has perhaps never happened that a social order founded upon one principle could transform itself by the adoption of another without passing through a phase of dissolution, it is conceivable that some great spirit, grasping in its chief implications the Socratic principle, might have so wrought it into education and into the popular mind that it should gradually have united the separate states of Greece into a great, free federal republic, fitted to lead the civilization of the world for a thousand years. Had Socrates founded a school and sent forth its members as apostles with the definite mission to announce the advent of the kingdom of liberty, in which each subject should recognize

the state as the embodiment of his own rationality,
and therefore the condition of his own freedom, it
seems as if such a result might have actually been
reached.   But neither Socrates himself nor any one of
his immediate followers was able to fathom the meaning of his principle sufficiently for this.

How little that principle was understood even by
the most gifted of his pupils is shown by the political
scheme worked out and advocated by Plato in his two
great works, the *Republic* and the *Laws*.   It is not my
purpose to offer a detailed analysis of either of these,
but to point out, in a general way, how the philosophic
state shaped itself in his mind, what education he
deemed necessary for it, and what practical results
followed from it.

In working out his scheme Plato misinterpreted—
no doubt, he believed he improved upon—the Socratic
principle in two ways.   The assertion that the principle of social union is universal intelligence he first
translated into the aphorism, " The state is the individual writ large."   Then, having converted the state
into a great individual, he degraded its human members into mere organs, or rather into cells composing
the organs of it.   From this all the rest of his political
theory follows naturally.   The state, he says, is a large
individual.   Now, the conditions of individual well-
being are the health and harmony of his faculties or
powers.   These powers are three : (1) intelligence ($νοῦς$),
having its acropolis in the head ; (2) courage or spirit
($θυμός$), encamped in the breast ; and (3) appetite ($τὸ$
$ἐπιθυμητικόν$), lodged in the abdomen.   Each of these
has its proper function, which, when duly performed,
constitutes its excellence or worth ($ἀρετή$).   The worth

10

of intelligence is prudence (φρόνησις); that of spirit, fortitude (ἀνδρεία); and that of appetite, temperance (σωφροσύνη). The harmony of all these is justice (δικαι- οσύνη), which, as combining the others, may be regarded as the basis of individual well-being. These four worths are what have been since Plato's time regarded as the "four cardinal virtues." They are primarily attributes not of relations between man and man, but between the faculties of the individual man. Regarding the state as a great individual, Plato now looks for the three human faculties in it, and finds them in three orders or classes of persons. As the organ of intelli- gence he finds the new philosophic class; as that of spirit, the military class; and as that of appetite, the in- dustrial class. When each of these performs its func- tion healthily and in harmony with the other two, there result political justice and social well-being. In this system the whole of the directing and organizing power is in the hands of the philosophers. The sol- diers are merely their agents, while the workers or wealth-producers are the slaves of both.

With respect to this ideal polity there are five points that deserve attention : (1) it is founded upon a crude metaphor; (2) we are nowhere told how it is to be evolved out of existing conditions; (3) it is founded upon truths accessible to only a small and exceptionally gifted portion of mankind ; (4) it takes no account of human affection or individual weal, and therefore deals with only an abstract fragment of man; consequently, (5) instead of being a means to freedom, it is an organ of the most complete des- potism that can be imagined. Let us consider these points in turn.

1. Plato's *Republic* is founded upon a crude metaphor. It is only the loosest kind of thinking that speaks of the state as an individual or an organism. That Plato should have been entrapped by such a metaphor need not surprise us, however, when we remember that the very same metaphor still plays a great and baneful part in much of our political and economic thinking. We still hear a great deal about the "social organism," the "social body," the "body politic"; and on these and similar metaphors, taken literally, many imposing and influential theories, that pass for science, are built up. But Plato's political system is not the only one that is founded upon a metaphor. Many influences and movements of even a far wider reach have no other or nobler origin. The whole ancient and mediæval theory of cognition, which influences much of our thinking even today, is based upon a material metaphor which makes knowledge arise from the complete fusion of the knowing and the known. To know a thing is to be it—τὸ γὰρ αὐτὸ νοεῖν ἐστίν τε καὶ εἶναι, as Parmenides said. In a similar way nearly all our modern philosophy, with all its Humean and Kantian skepticisms, all its Hegelian subjectless processes, and all its Comtean and Spencerian phenomenalism, has its origin in Locke's metaphor, which makes knowledge consist of impressions similar to those made by a seal upon wax. And in the department of theology there is much of the same sort.

2. We are nowhere told how the new polity is to be evolved out of existing circumstances. The *Republic* is a work of art, and has all the characteristics of such. It presents a sculpturesque group in

a static condition. It reveals neither past growth nor future progress. Like all Utopian schemes, it fails to take any account of that very evolution which is the life of society. It has nothing to say about the material out of which, or the method by which, the new order is to develop itself, nothing about any principle or goal of progress whereby its life is to be guided. It comes from nowhere, and it goes nowhere. There is here a capital defect. To any scheme of social regeneration which is other than a mere dream two conditions, above all others, are essential: (1) that it shall take full account of the conditions to which it is to be applied—the grade of intelligence, the desires, aims, and ideals of the people whom it undertakes to elevate; (2) that it shall make continuous struggle and progress possible by exhibiting an aim or ideal calculated to enlist universal interest and energy. Failing, as it did, to fulfill either of these conditions, Plato's *Republic* remained a mere dream, encouraging a tendency, always common enough, to separate theory from practice, and to make a fantastic picture of social perfection do duty for a sustained effort at social amelioration. Thus it not only contributed to alienate its readers from the institutions about them, but also to encourage a fantastic and unpractical spirit in them.

3. It is founded upon truths accessible to only a small and exceptionally gifted portion of mankind. It is in this respect that it diverges most widely from the principles of Socrates, and introduces notions to which he was apparently an entire stranger. This is a crucial point, and one that, therefore, deserves close consideration. Socrates had held that all truth was implicit in the human mind, and required only the

obstetric dialectic (that is, conversational) process to make it explicit. When explicit, it proved to be the same in all men, and for this reason could serve as the principle of political freedom. In yielding submission to the truth common to all men, the individual was only loyal to himself, and therefore free. And it is perfectly obvious that this is the only condition under which political freedom is possible. From this position of Socrates Plato entirely—we might almost say fatally—departed. According to him, truth, instead of being implicit in the human mind, and in every human mind, is not in the mind at all, but lies, in the form of self-existent ideas, in a region above the heavens,* to which only a small portion of mankind can ever hope to have access, since only a small portion are capable of climbing the giddy dialectic stair that leads thereto.

It is not difficult to see the momentousness of this change of view. If a state is to be based upon truth, and truth lies where only a few exceptional men can reach it, it follows at once (1) that no such thing as freedom is possible for men; (2) that the organization and management of the state must be left to those few men who are able to catch a glimpse of the heaven of truth. Plato, like the idealist he was, shrinks from neither of these conclusions. On the contrary, he embodies both of them in his *Republic*, in which there is no freedom for any one, but in which the philosophers rule without laws and without responsibility to anybody but God. As Plato's ideal state was never realized, these two conclusions did no immediate practical harm. But there followed from

---

* *Phædrus,* 247 C.

his view of the nature and location of truth others that had far more profound and pervasive consequences. Since truth lies outside the mind, it can not, of course, be evolved by any mental process, but must come to it, if at all, through some sort of experience, which the individual may or may not have. Those who have it must, of necessity, possess a special faculty for the apprehension of eternal and immutable ideas—what might be called a supernatural sense. To this sense Plato gives the name of love (ἔρως) or frenzy (μανία), a divine element in the soul, which in its undeveloped condition seizes upon the beautiful in its most material manifestations, but which, in proportion as it is trained, rises to more and more spiritual forms of beauty, until at last it reaches the beautiful itself, which is one with the good—that is, God.* This is the faculty which sees divine things. Its action is expressed by the verb θεωρεῖν and the noun θεωρία, which Plato assumed to be derived from τὰ θεῖα ὁρᾶν, and to which accordingly he gave this meaning.† In a passage already alluded to (*Phædrus*, 247 C *sqq.*) we read: " This supercelestial region no earthly poet

---

* See the closing sentences of Plotinus' tract *On the Beautiful, Enneads*, I, 6. Plotinus fairly enough interprets Plato here.

† Trendelenburg, *Element. Log. Aristot.*, says: " Already in Plato θεωρεῖν is transferred from an attentive, passive looking at divine things or games to a contemplation of the true with all the energy of the mind (alta mente)." In Aristotle, *Metaph.*, Λ, 1072b, 23 *sq.*, the above etymology is obviously assumed, and Simplicius, commenting upon the passage, says: " Of all parts of the intellect, the divinest is theory (θεωρία)." Compare Alexander of Aphrodisias, Comment. on *Analyt. Pri.*, Scholia to Berlin edition, p. 141b, 2 *sq.*; and Suidas, *Lexicon, sub voc.* θεωρία.

has ever sung, or ever will sing, worthily; but it is of
this sort. We need surely have no hesitation about
telling the truth, especially since truth is the very
thing we are talking about. So, then, the colorless,
formless, intangible essence, which essentially is, which
is visible only to the pilot intellect, and which is the
object of all true science, inhabits this region. The
mind of God, being fed with intellect and pure science, and beholding Being after a space, *loves* it, and,
contemplating (θεωροῦσα) the truth, is nourished and
made happy until the revolution brings it back to the
same point in the circle. In this revolution it sees
justice itself (absolute justice), it sees temperance, it
sees science—science not as it is with the addition of
becoming, nor under the various aspects in which it
occurs in what we call being, but as it is in that
which is essentially being. . . . And this is the life of
the gods. As to the other souls, that which most no-
bly follows and resembles God, raises the head of its
charioteer into the outer region and is carried round
with the revolution, although disconcerted by the
horses, and beholding with difficulty the things that
are; whereas that which sometimes rises above and
sometimes sinks below, through the intractability of
the horses, sees some things and fails to see others.
And all the rest, though they follow with a hanker-
ing for the upper region, are borne round in an impotent, waterlogged condition, treading each other
down and running against each other in their effort
to get ahead of each other."

It may be said that all this is allegory, mere metaphor, and, indeed, so it is; but it is allegory that was
taken literally by Plato's followers, and, as so taken,

exercised a vast influence upon thought. And even to Plato himself it is not all allegory. It is his serious belief that the ideas which constitute true knowledge have their abode in a supercelestial—that is, supernatural—world, accessible to only a few exceptional souls naturally endowed with a divine faculty of clear-eyed love, which they have trained and developed through the practice of dialectics. This combination of love and dialectics is certainly curious enough, and is to be understood only if we regard dialectics as merely the means whereby the soul discovers higher and higher objects for its love. The faculty which grasps and appropriates these objects is not dialectics, but love or frenzy. " The greatest of blessings come to us through frenzy, provided it is given with a divine giving," Socrates is made to say.*

It would be impossible to insist too strongly upon this point in Plato's system, since it is fraught with the most momentous consequences, and, indeed, is the one which gives to that system its chief interest and importance. In one word, Plato, by placing truth in a supernatural world, accessible only through a faculty of divine frenzy, became the founder of mysticism, which is the very essence of spiritual religion, and which as such has played an overwhelming part in the world's history.

Historians of philosophy, in treating of Neoplatonism, are often at a loss to discover whence that system drew the mystic element which is so prominent in it, and are usually inclined to credit it to the religions of the East. It seems to me that this is a mistake, for two reasons : (1) because these religions, so far as I can

---

* *Phœdrus*, 244 A.

see, had nothing which corresponds to the mysticism of Neoplatonism; and (2) because that mysticism is to be found without difficulty in the writings of Plato. As to the former of these, while it may, and perhaps must, be admitted that Neoplatonism contained a magic, or theurgic, and mantic element derived from Eastern sources, and that this came to be connected with the mystic element, still it is clear enough that the two elements are different, and have different origins. The truth is, they stand related to each other as nature-religion does to spirit-religion, as necessity to freedom. Their union has played a great part in religion for the last two thousand years. It gave rise to just those elements in the Roman Catholic Church against which Protestantism was a revolt. Protestantism tried to separate mysticism from theurgy, and, while dropping the latter, to retain the former. At all events, it seems clear enough that the origin of spiritual mysticism, as distinct from material theurgy and mantic, is to be sought nowhere but in Plato's doctrine of self-subsistent ideas, and that Neoplatonism was, in a far higher degree than is generally conceded, a genuine continuation of Platonism.

It seems, then, that Plato's great achievement consisted not in drawing up a scheme of an ideal state upon Socratic principles, but in introducing into philosophy the notion of a faculty of apprehension higher than sense, in fact (to use a modern phrase), the faculty of the supernatural. The scheme, as such, never had any appreciable effect upon political institutions, though it hovered long as an ideal before unpractical minds; but the mystic principle, which lay at the bottom of it, proved a leaven which brought a ferment into every department of Greek life, and, above all, into education, until at last it found embodiment in an institution which was not a state at all, but a church.* How far Plato was aware of the difference between his own principle and that of Socrates we can not tell; but certain it is that instead of carrying on the work of Socrates, he interrupted it and began a work of his own.

We need not here consider the various forms which the mystic element in Plato's thought assumed in later times—in Neopythagoreanism, Neoplatonism, and Christianity. In his own time and the century following it manifested itself in the form of a tendency to turn away from the affairs and interests of this world, and to look for happiness in the contemplation of things eternal. Instead, therefore, of inducing men to strive after a higher form of social life (if, indeed, that proposed by Plato *was* a higher form), his influence went to withdraw them more and more from social or, at all events, political life, and to make them feel that their true citizenship was in the invisible world. If a

---

* In taking this view of Plato's achievement, I am happy to find myself in agreement with Dr. Gideon Spicker, who in his recent work, *Die Ursachen des Verfalls der Philosophie, in alter und neuer Zeit,* says in regard to the mystic element in Neoplatonism: "Since this mysticism professes to be, more than anything else, a renewal of Plato, we are justified in surmising that his philosophy contains an element akin to this direction of feeling" (p. 112). And he goes on to point out the presence of this element in Plato. This work of Spicker's is especially important as emphasizing the fact that the supernatural sense, first brought to light by Plato, is essential to the existence not only of religion, but also of philosophy, which without it always degenerates into rationalism, and thence into skepticism.

state could not be founded upon mystic vision, there was nothing—so at least it seemed—to prevent the individual from attaining this vision for himself, and communicating the content of it to his fellows.

We have seen that the gradual encroachment of diagogic life tended to weaken men's interest in practical life. Plato's *Republic* was an attempt to show how the two might be reconciled, and the former made to contribute to the perfection of the latter. *Diagoge* was to be confined to the few elect souls capable of rising to a contemplation of eternal ideas, and these were to convey the content of that vision to the less favored majority of mankind for its guidance. The attempt not only failed, but it contributed to aggravate the very evil—viz., individualism—which it was intended to cure. The effect of all this upon education was very marked. The education which had aimed at making good citizens was spurned by men who sought only to be guided to the vision of divine things. Hence the old gymnastics and music fell into disrepute, their place being taken by dialectics and philosophy, which latter Plato makes even Socrates call "the highest music." * Similarly dialectics came to be regarded as the highest gymnastics.

4. Plato's *Republic* takes no account of human affection or individual will, and therefore deals with only an abstract fragment of man. This is the common fault of all the authors of Utopian systems from Plato

---

* *Phædo*, IV, 61 A. Compare Chap. IX : "Those who lay hold of philosophy properly and successfully run the risk of being misunderstood by the rest of the world, which does not see that the sole object of their study is to die and to be in the state of the dead " (ἀποθνήσκειν τε καὶ τεθνάναι).

onward. They treat men as if they were fragments of glass to be arranged into a pleasing mosaic, embodying some theoretic idea coming from outside. In the case of the *Republic* it was supposed to come directly from God, and to be communicated to philosophers, who were thus commissioned to construct and keep in order the social mosaic without any regard to the affections or will of its component parts. Men's affections, to a large extent, are directed upon home (which implies property), wife, and children, and their wills seek to select their own environment and sphere of activity. All these objects Plato would take away. The citizen of his *Republic* is to have neither home, property, wife, nor child for his affections, nor any choice with regard to his own surroundings or occupation. It is, of course, entirely unfair to say that Plato champions community of property and wives. In his scheme there is no place for either. When the state requires children, it breeds them as it would cattle, and rears them with as little regard to their parents as if they were chickens hatched from stolen eggs. When it requires material means, it calls upon the producers of wealth to furnish it; they exist for that purpose. When children are born according to state regulations, they are taken possession of by state officials, and if they seem vigorous and free from defect, they are placed in public institutions to be educated; otherwise they are destroyed. The education to which they are now subjected is in its main features the same as that current in Greece in Plato's time. But it is carried further; its component parts are differently emphasized; and, above all, it has a different aim, as far at least as the individual is concerned.

Whereas the current education aimed at producing capable citizens, practical, active, and patriotic, that of Plato seeks to develop philosophers, whose home and chief interest are in the invisible world. Those children who prove incapable of higher instruction are soon relegated to the industrial class, whose aim is supposed to be having, not being. The others continue their curriculum till about the age of thirty, when those who show no special aptitude for dialectics, but seem active and brave, are assigned to the soldier class, the few that give evidence of higher capabilities proceeding with their studies until, having attained the divine vision, they are admitted to the ruling philosophic class. In all this individual affection and will are completely ruled out.

5. Plato's *Republic*, instead of being a means to freedom, is an organ of the most complete despotism. This follows directly from what has been said under the last two headings. Any form of government which is based upon mystical principles inaccessible to the individual reason and imposed (*octroyés*) from without, and which disregards individual affections and will, is of necessity a despotism, no matter what title it may assume, what lofty sanctions it may claim for itself. This has been clearly shown in the case of religious politics claiming to be based on divine revelation. For all these Plato's *Republic* furnished the model.*

---

* It is no part of the purpose of this work to give an account of Plato's system in detail, its provision for the education of women and their equality with men, the mode of life pursued by philosophers and soldiers, etc. For these I must refer the reader to my work on *Aristotle and the Ancient Educational Ideals.*

The appearance of that work forms an epoch in human history and education. In the latter, indeed, it did not cause any sudden change; but its influence gradually sapped the old system and the old ideal, and substituted others for them. Education ceased to be political, and became either philosophical or rhetorical; and precisely the same thing was true of art, which is always an expression of current education. To see this it is only necessary to compare the dramas of Æschylus, which are political, with those of Euripides, which are philosophical *and* rhetorical, or the works of Phidias, such as the Athena Parthenos, with those of Scopas and Praxiteles—e. g., the Niobe Group and the Olympian Hermes. As political education decayed, those persons who found themselves unfit for philosophy betook themselves to rhetoric, which was the continuation of sophistic, bearing the same relation to the teaching of the Sophists as dialectic did to that of Socrates and Plato. The rhetorical schools were always the rivals of the philosophical, and had an exactly opposite tendency. Just as philosophic education tended to suppress individualism and make men feel that they were but parts of a great whole, so rhetorical education, true to its origin, tended to emphasize and re-enforce it by producing clever, versatile, self-centered men of the world, capable of making their way anywhere by address, subtlety, and readiness. Both kinds of education were equally inimical to the political life of Greece, the one substituting for the state, as the center of interest, God; the other, the individual.

Under these circumstances we need not be surprised that the Athenian state gradually fell into decay, and became an easy prey to the semi-barbarous Macedonians, in whom the Aryan instinct of personal loyalty took the place of political feeling. No state will ever be strong which is not regarded by its citizens either as the supreme object of interest and effort, or as necessary to the realization of such object. And whenever either religion or individualism becomes the supreme interest, the state must fall into decay, unless it can show that it is essential to the success of the tendency which is in the ascendant. It is always safest when it can show that it is indispensable to both.*

With all this we must not forget that when Greece, as a political power, decayed, the education and the history of the Greek people were very far from being at an end. Indeed, there is a sense in which it may be said that their history was only beginning. Plato and Aristotle were right when they looked upon the small Greek states as schools; and the real manhood of the Greeks, their active influence on the great world, began only when they had graduated from these and left them behind. No doubt there is something very attractive about the Greek pedagogic states, and they graduated some incomparable people, particularly in the days of Marathon and Salamis; but, after all, they only furnished the necessary preparation for the work which the Greeks were destined to accomplish in the world, in the spheres of art, science, philosophy, and religion. This work began only when the small pedagogical polities of Greece were going to pieces. We

---

* It argued a profound insight on the part of Constantine that, when the Church had become men's chief object of interest, he sought to save the empire by connecting the two, and making the latter seem essential to the former.

all admire the patriotic eloquence of Demosthenes, and are almost inclined to weep over the conquest of Greece by the semi-barbarous Macedonians under Philip and Alexander; but Demosthenes' attempt was a romantic, Quixotic enterprise, an effort to swim against the stream of history; and the conquest of Greece was precisely what was needed in order to make the Greeks set about their appointed task of educating the world, instead of wasting their powers in babblings and squabblings among themselves.

It was through the work done by Socrates and Plato that the Greeks were enabled to complete the education which prepared them for their mission. It was through this that they were able to substitute for their old ethnic religion, upon which their little exclusive states had been built up, and upon which only such states *could* be built up, a religious principle upon which a world-wide institution could be reared. And no sooner had they attained this principle than they became the bearers of it to all the world—at first, indeed, unconsciously, but later on consciously. Like Socrates, Plato had "builded better than he knew." In seeking to construct a little Grecian polity upon philosophic principles, he had utterly failed; his *Republic* was a wild dream which only dreamers could ever think of trying to realize, or indeed desire to see realized; but in working it out he had discovered a principle which was destined to be the form of something far higher, something which it would have been impossible for him to imagine. We may sum up the work of Socrates and Plato by saying that the former discovered the principle of the universal state, the latter the principle of the universal Church; the former the principle of moral liberty, the latter the principle of unity with God. In this sense, and only in this sense, can it be said that Plato carried on the work of Socrates. Thus these two men together not only prepared the way for the transition from particularism to universalism in politics, but also initiated a separation between the civil and religious institutions which had been confounded in the old states. It is of course true that there was, strictly speaking, no Church, even in the larger Hellenic world, for four centuries after Plato; but it is likewise true that the *form* of the Church came into existence in Plato's lifetime, and only waited for a living content to become a reality. That content was the realization of the mystic vision of which Plato had dreamed.* We are therefore prepared to find that after Plato there grew up, alongside the state, societies based upon this vision, the so-called philosophic schools. While the followers of Socrates owned no social bond, those of Plato, Aristotle, Zeno, Epicurus, and all the great system-builders form themselves into schools; and these are the forerunners and, in large degree, the models for the church-congregations, at least in the pagan world.† The history of these schools is, from the date of their rise, the most important part of the history of Greece. It was through these that she exerted upon the world that influence which constitutes her historic importance.

---

* See Bratuschek's lecture on *Die Bedeutung der platonischen Philosophie für die religiösen Fragen der Gegenwart*, Berlin, 1873.

† The Jewish Christian Church, with its "prophesying," was something very different from the Gentile Church with its

In treating of Plato's attempt to evolve the plan of a state founded on philosophical principles we have confined our attention solely to the *Republic*. But this embodies only one of the attempts he made. Another, and one differing in many important respects from the former, is presented to us in the *Laws*, a work which seems to have been written in his declining years, when the impracticability of his earlier scheme had become apparent to him. It is a work of far less literary merit than the *Republic*, but it is hardly less interesting. Its relation to the latter may be made clear by a simple consideration. The aim of Socrates' efforts had been to find a principle by which the anarchic individualism of sophistic teaching might be overcome. He did so by discovering the existence of universal reason in man. Plato, by substituting for this his supermental ideas, whose civic embodiment could be only a despotic state, passed to the opposite extreme—viz., to the exaggerated socialism of Pythagoras. Having in his *Republic* practically indorsed this, he was led by degrees to a more careful study of Pythagoreanism itself and its practical results. So deeply did this study affect him that he finally, to a large extent, departed

---

preaching, which is altogether of Greek origin, being borrowed from the philosophical and rhetorical schools. (See Hatch, *Hibbert Lectures*, 1888, pp. 107–109.) To the form and ceremonial of the Gentile Church there went, no doubt, important elements derived from the Jewish synagogue and the Greek mysteries; but the supernatural and spiritual bond, which is the essential principle of the Church, existed already in the Greek philosophic schools. It might, indeed, be maintained that the synagogue itself owed its origin to Greek influence. It certainly arose when that influence was at its highest in Palestine.

from the principles of Socrates and embraced those of Pythagoras. The result was the *Laws*, in which alone of all Plato's works Socrates does not appear.

Two circumstances seem to have contributed to bring about this change: (1) the growing social disorder in Greece, against which the scheme propounded in the *Republic* was obviously ineffective; (2) the manifest impotence of ideas as ethical sanctions. Lengthened experience gradually convinced Plato of two things: (1) that society can be reformed only through the forces by which it has been built up and is still maintained, never by principles imported from without; (2) that the most important of these forces is religion with its gods, a force for which metaphysics, with its ideas, is no substitute. Without, therefore, denying—nay, indeed, still affirming—that the *Republic* presents the ultimate ideal state, he admits that such a state is possible only when the citizens are "gods or sons of gods," * and then proceeds to draw out the plan of a state which, as being based upon the forces at work in society, and especially upon religion and the gods, might seem to offer more promise of realization. Accordingly, in the *Laws*, the ideas of the *Republic* are replaced by the popular gods, the mystic vision by popular good sense (φρόνησις), the philosophic class by (1) a hereditary prince, (2) a commissioner of public education and a senate chosen by vote, and (3) a body of officials determined by lot, and, finally, the industrial class by slaves and resident foreigners. Of his previous three classes the only one

---

* Εἴτε που θεοὶ ἢ παῖδες θεῶν, *Laws*, 739 D. See the whole passage, and mark the expression "sons of gods."

that remains is the military. All these changes are
concessions to the real, and it is manifest that Plato
in making them has abandoned the ideal standpoint
and placed himself on a basis of history and experience.

By nothing is this shown more clearly than by the
part which the gods and their worship play in the new
scheme. Mature reflection upon popular ethical sanctions and an acquaintance with the results of Pythagorean teaching had convinced him that among men
no social or political order was possible that was not
based upon religion and the worship of gods, acknowledged to be real personalities. Accordingly, he lays down
the most detailed rules for the worship of the accepted
gods,* demons, and heroes, and ordains that any word
or act, on the part of any citizen, showing disrespect
for divine things shall be punished in the most rigorous way. He goes even much further than this. Iden-
tifying certain of the gods with the heavenly bodies, or,
as Dante would say, with the intelligences that move
the spheres, and conceiving that much of the order of
things on the earth is due to their influence, he practically makes astrology an essential part of religion,
and the worship of the " hosts of heaven " † part of
religious ritual. And this ritual, in consequence, became not only extremely detailed and complicated—in-

---

* Οἱ κατὰ νόμον ὄντες θεοί, *Laws*, X, 904 A. Cf. *Golden Words*,
line 1, θεοὺς, νόμῳ ὡς διάκεινται.

† Whence Plato derived his astrological notions I am unable
to say, whether from Pythagoras or directly from the Egyptians,
Babylonians, or Phœnicians ; but it seems to me that the notion
of introducing astrology into religion was in all probability due
to Pythagorean influence.

asmuch as each deity, dæmon, and hero had to be worshiped with certain fixed rites, performed at stated
seasons, and with no other—but also theurgic and
mantic, as indeed every religion necessarily does that
pays homage to the host of heaven or to nature-powers
of any sort.

This view of the relation of the heavenly powers or
bodies to the affairs of life introduced a great change
in education. Whereas in the *Republic* education had
culminated in dialectics leading to the vision of super-
sensual ideas, in the *Laws* it culminates in the mathe-
matical sciences—arithmetic, geometry, and astronomy
—the first two being mainly preparatory to the last.
It need not be said that for Plato astronomy is astrology, whence, in recommending the study of the mathe-
matical sciences, he does so in the interest of religion,
or, more strictly speaking, of superstition. Mathematics are to be studied in order that we may place
ourselves in the proper relation to the stellar intelligences.*

In the political scheme set forth in the *Laws* a
place is, of course, found for the family and for private property; but into details like these we can not
enter, our purpose being merely to show how the work
affected the education of the Greek people—that is,
what elements it introduced into their thought. And
this may be stated in a few words. Inasmuch as the
scheme propounded in the *Laws* is little more than a

---

* "This is what I say is incumbent both upon our citizens
and upon our young men with respect to the gods in the heavens,
that they should learn so much about them all as not to utter
blasphemy about them, but to treat them always reverently, in
sacrifices and pious prayers."—*Laws*, VII, 821 D. E.

compound of the constitutions of Athens and Sparta, sanctioned by a religion bordering closely upon Sabæanism, it is obvious that it is mainly in this last element that the novelty of the *Laws* consists. Nor is this a small matter if we consider it in its consequences. Let us do so.

The tendency of the teaching of Socrates, as well as of that of Plato in the *Republic*, had been to draw men away from the old nature-divinities of polytheism, and to direct their attention upon a single principle, as governing the universe—in a word, to turn them to monotheism. And, indeed, had the fundamental thought of Socrates been faithfully carried out to its legitimate consequences, it is hard to see what other result could have been reached than a spiritual monotheism, since that is the necessary presupposition of all "idiopsychological ethics" (to use an excellent expression of Dr. Martineau's). But, as we have seen, no such good fortune befell the thought of Socrates. Plato substituted for it one of his own, which did not, and could not, lead to a spiritual monotheism, but, at best, only to a mono-ideism, such as Hegel afterward reached; and when he found this inadequate to furnishing a principle for the reorganization of society, he had no resource but to fall back into material polytheism, which he then attempted to raise to the height of a moral sanction by connecting it with a crude physical theory and with a worship consisting mainly of theurgic or magic rites and divination. It was due mainly to Plato that the Greeks, in their effort to find a true moral sanction, were left to choose between a lifeless abstraction called "the Good" and a crude material polytheism, and that they thus missed the "living God," whom Socrates, and before him the prophetic Æschylus, came so near finding.

We have already seen that the adoption of the former of these alternatives was the source of that mysticism which played such a large part in subsequent philosophy and religion. We can now see that the adoption of the latter gave currency and respectability to the theurgic, magic, and mantic rites which to this day have maintained themselves in much of the religion of the civilized world. No doubt these rites existed in all nature-religions, not excepting that of Greece; but they would, in all probability, have disappeared soon after the time of Socrates, at least from the religion of thinking men, had they not received prestige and a fresh lease of life from the authority of Plato. Thus they came to be perpetuated, and thus it was that the religion of the thoughtful Greeks after Plato's time was, to a large extent, a compound of a lofty mysticism, striving after the beatific vision of a bald abstraction, and a crude material superstition, expressing itself in magic ceremonies. Such was the result of Plato's attempt to found a social order upon abstract philosophic principles.

CHAPTER VII.

PLATO's attempt to found a state on the mystic
vision of divine ideas, whatever its more remote results, was a failure; and of this he himself became
ultimately so well aware that he attempted to found
one upon popular superstition. This likewise was
necessarily a failure, so that at the death of Plato the
task which Socrates had undertaken remained unac-
complished, and the principle of social union which
he had discovered undeveloped and unapplied. But
in elaborating his second scheme Plato had made use
of a principle which, had he known how to take full
advantage of it, might have helped him to a better
result—the principle that all social reform must come
from a wise direction of the immanent forces by which
society is built up. The full comprehension and application of this principle were left for Aristotle.

This philosopher abandoned the position of Plato
without returning to that of Socrates. Without altogether setting aside Platonic ideas, he freed them from
many of the difficulties that attached to them as conceived by Plato. By treating their separate existence

in a supercelestial world as pure mythology, and planting them as organizing forces in the material world, and as concepts in the intellect—realized in the divine; potential, and realizable in the human—he prepared the way for the conclusion that if divine ideas are ever to be found at all, they must be looked for in nature and in mind. In nature they are seen on their external side, in the form of becoming; in mind, on their internal side, in the form of being; and they are adequately seen only when the two sides are simultaneously presented. These ideas, in so far as they relate to human practice, appear on their inner side as ethical ends or motives; on their outer, as social institutions, and these two must be seen in their correlation, if ever a theory of practice is to be reached, and practice itself place upon a secure footing.

According to Aristotle, all intelligent action is action for the sake of an end, which may be defined as "the Good" (τὸ ἀγαθόν). The good of man is Happiness (εὐδαιμονία), which consists in the realization of his highest or distinguishing faculty—viz., intellect. In his *Ethics* Aristotle seeks to show how the individual must discipline himself in order to reach this end, while in the *Politics* he undertakes to present the external, the social, and economic conditions under which such discipline promises to be most successful. Thus for Aristotle, as for Plato, the state is primarily a school of virtue, and the supreme virtue consists in the exercise of the intellect.

In both the *Ethics* and the *Politics* Aristotle goes to work inductively. In the former, after defining the nature of "the Good," he proceeds to classify the virtues and the vices, and to show how each is related to that Good—the former conducing to it, the latter leading away from it. In the latter he considers the various forms of government and their relation to each other, as well as to the characters, temperaments, and culture of different peoples.* These do not concern us at present. We have only to consider what he conceives the function of the state to be in educating men so that they may reach "the Good." In trying to define this, he begins with a very sharp and, on the whole, very just criticism of the socialistic doctrines propounded in Plato's *Republic* and *Laws*. He points out the fallacy involved in the conception of the state as the individual writ large, and emphatically denies the truth of the doctrine that a state is better in proportion as it approximates perfect unity. On the contrary, he says, the more completely a thing is a unity, the less self-sufficient, the less capable of prolonging its existence it is. If we reflect that the individual is more of a unity than the family, and the family than the state, we shall see that unity and self-sufficiency are in inverse ratio to each other. Moreover, when the state is regarded as an individual the happiness of the whole will be aimed at, and not that of the parts— a hand or a foot. But to talk of the happiness of a state, as something possible apart from the happiness of the human beings that compose it, is to talk nonsense. Happiness is not like evenness in number. A number may be even though all its components are

---

* His review of the different forms of government was based upon a very wide induction. Before undertaking it he wrote out the "constitutions" of two hundred and fifty (some say two hundred and fifty-eight) different states. One of these, the "Constitution of the Athenians," has recently been discovered.

odd (units); but a state can not be happy if its members are unhappy, as those of the Platonic state are. Aristotle shows further not only that the Platonic state could not possibly be realized, but also that if it were, it would neither obviate the evils nor secure the blessings which he believes it would. He points out specially the evils that would arise from community of wives or property, and shows that they would far overbalance the advantages.

It might seem from this criticism that Aristotle would be prepared to reverse the Platonic doctrine that the individual exists for the state, and to say that the state exists for the individual. But he is both too much of a Greek and too much of a philosopher to do this. He maintains that man and the state do not stand to each other in the relation of end and means, but are essentially correlates. "Man is *by nature* a political animal," and the notion of a man without a state (ἄπολις) is as absurd as that of a state without a man. He even commits himself to the paradox that the state is prior to the individual,* by which he means that it is man's civic nature by which his individual manhood is rendered possible. It is through the state that man is man. Without the state he would have to be a beast or a god. In one aspect, therefore, the relation of the individual to the state is organic, in another it is federal. It is this combination of the organic and the federal that constitutes the political. A polity is more than an organism,† more than an individual how-

---

* Ἡ πόλις καὶ φύσει καὶ πρότερον ἢ ἕκαστος, *Pol.*, I, 2, 1253a 25.

† It is curious how long it has taken the world—nay, how long it has taken political thinkers—to rise to Aristotle's point

ever large we may write him. I am not aware that
Aristotle has anywhere hazarded the assertion that a
unity is always higher in proportion to the independence of the elements which it unites, and that the
highest possible unity would be one whose elements
were absolutely independent; but there can be no
doubt that this follows from his teaching, and would
have been cheerfully admitted by him. To convince
ourselves that he held this view with respect to political unities we have only to read the second chapter
of the second book of the *Politics*, where, in dealing
with the question of communism and private property,
he maintains that, while possession ought to be private,
the citizens of a community should be so well educated
as to be ready to use their wealth for the public weal.
" And to see that they have this education is the proper
task of the legislator." * Obviously, therefore, the
business of the state is not to make its citizens dependent parts of a whole, as Plato had held, but to
develop in them moral wills, and thereby to make
them independent. In a word, Aristotle regards the
state as a *moral* unity, whose principle is free will, and
is therefore the determined foe of all state-socialism.
In the ideal state men would be absolutely free.
Of the state-forms capable of realization among men

---

of view in this matter. We still hear the state spoken of as an
organism, and theories propounded with regard to it as if it
really were so. See, for example, Bluntschli, *Theory of the
State*, p. 12 *sqq.* (Eng. trans.). This writer even goes so far as to
maintain that the state is masculine and the Church feminine !
Ibid., p. 22 *sq.*

* ῞Οπως δὲ γίνωνται τοιοῦτοι, τοῦ νομοθέτου τοῦτ᾽ ἔργον ἴδιόν ἐστιν.
Pol., ii, 5, 1263a 39 *sq.*

such as they are, that is the best and highest which allows the individual the greatest possible amount of liberty.

In seeking to discover what form of state best accomplishes this, Aristotle classifies and passes in review all the forms of government with which he is acquainted, or which he conceives possible, and finds that there are in all six of them—three good and three bad (παρεκβάσεις). The difference between a good and a bad government is that, while the former aims at the good of the whole people, the latter seeks that of a class. The good governments are—(1) Monarchy, in which one rules; (2) aristocracy, in which some (the best) rule; and (3) constitutional republic (πολιτεία), in which all rule. The bad governments corresponding respectively to these are—(1) Tyranny, (2) oligarchy, (3) democracy. The difference between the last two, however, is not so much a matter of number as of wealth. Oligarchy is government by the rich; democracy, by the poor. In arranging these governments in an order of descending goodness, Aristotle applies the principle that "the corruption of the best is the worst." * The result is: (1) Monarchy, (2) aristocracy, (3) constitutional republic, (4) democracy, (5) oligarchy, (6) tyranny.

---

* "*Corruptio optimi pessima est.*" In this generalized form it became an adage in Scholastic philosophy. Dante (*Purg.*, xxx, 118 *sqq.*) and Shakespeare ("Lilies that fester smell far worse than weeds," *Son.*, xciv, 14) both adopt it. In its original form it was applied to governments—"the corruption of the first and most divine must be the worst" (ἀνάγκη γὰρ τὴν μὲν τῆς πρώτης καὶ θειοτάτης παρέκβασιν εἶναι χειρίστην, *Pol.*, iv, 2, 1289a 39 *sqq.*).

According to Aristotle, then, monarchy is the best form of government for educating men to freedom, and tyranny the worst. This conclusion was due not to any philosophic reasoning from abstract principles, or to any preconception of human nature, but to experience, and, perhaps even in a larger degree than was justified, to the experience of his own time. The same social convulsion and confusion that had driven Plato to turn his back on all actual governments and construct his fantastic and impossible *Republic* were before Aristotle, and even in an aggravated form. But the effect upon him was altogether different from what it had been upon Plato; and the reason of this is not far to seek. While Plato, with his poetical tendencies, could find no refuge from the actual save in the abstract ideal, Aristotle, with his belief that the ideal was not abstract at all, looked for help in a larger and more comprehensive view of the real. And he was greatly aided in this by the circumstances of his life, which in this connection deserve careful consideration.

Though Aristotle spent a large part of his life— nearly thirty years in all—in Athens, and though, as his works clearly show, he took a deep and sympathetic interest in its government and people, he never was— never could be, and probably never even wished to be —anything more than a stranger or resident foreigner (μέτοικος) there. He was a Macedonian not only by birth, but, as many circumstances show, also in sympathy. He had seen the best side of the great Macedonian monarchs, and in his later life, when he was writing his *Politics*, he witnessed not only their easy and complete triumph over the democracies and oli-

garchies of Greece, but also their beneficent influence
in restoring peace, order, and prosperity to the whole
people.   Before his very eyes the monarchy of which
he was a subject proved itself not only stronger, but
more civilizing than any other form of government with
which he was acquainted.   Under these circumstances
it would have been strange indeed if, with his deep
respect for experience, he had not assigned to monarchy the first place among the forms of government.
At all events there can be no doubt that his experience
of the power and influence of Macedonia had a considerable part in shaping his political theories.

It seems at first sight strange that a man who laid
so much stress on the distinction between Greeks and
barbarians as Aristotle did should have shown so much
respect for the Macedonians, who were generally considered at least half barbarians; but it must be borne
in mind that a very large proportion of the subjects of
the Macedonian kings were pure-blooded Greeks, and
Greeks of a very superior type, and that both Philip
and Alexander had not only received a most careful
Greek education, but were proud to proclaim themselves the bearers and champions of Greek culture, a
claim which the Greeks themselves allowed when they
admitted them to participation in the Olympic games.
Thus the Greece of Aristotle was the Macedonian monarchy, of which the Greece of Plato was only a dependent province; and we can well imagine that the
battle of Chæronea, which to the latter must have
seemed the greatest of disasters, may have appeared
to Aristotle the dawn of a better order of things.   In
his recently discovered *Constitution of Athens* he
closes the history of that city with the restoration of

the democracy by Thrasybulus in B. C. 403, and does not even allude to the Macedonian conquest.

Aristotle's experiences with the Macedonian monarchy placed him in a difficult position, which is curiously but plainly manifested in his *Politics*. While he maintains that monarchy is, absolutely speaking, the highest form of government, and that aristocracy comes next to it, he nevertheless admits that, considering the difficulty of finding a real monarch or an aristocracy whose unselfishness can be depended on, the best form generally realizable is the constitutional republic. We can easily see that in making this admission he is influenced by the impression which Philip and Alexander had made upon him. Such men, he evidently believes, are not found every day, and can not be made to order. He is probably thinking of them when he describes the man whom he considers fit to be a monarch. "If," he says, "there be any one man, or some small number of men not large enough to constitute a state, so exceedingly transcendent in worth that neither the worth nor the political capacity of all the rest bears any comparison to his or theirs (as the case may be), such men are no longer to be considered part of the state; for it would be an injustice to place them on an equal footing with those who are so inferior to them in worth and political capacity. Nay, such a man must take the place of a god among men. Thus we see that wherever there is legislation it presupposes men generically and potentially equal, whereas the men just referred to are beyond the sphere of law; for they are the law; and certainly it would be ridiculous for any one to lay down laws for them. They would probably reply as Antisthenes said the

lions did when the hares and rabbits took to harangu-
ing in favor of equal rights for all." *

We can readily see that in accepting and propounding a doctrine like this Aristotle was standing on the
boundary line between two epochs and ideals of political life. On one side of him, stretching away into the
past, were the little pedagogic republics of Greece, with
their narrow interests, regulated lives, and intense,
supercilious patriotism; on the other, looming up in
the future, was a great Hellenic monarchy, with broad
interests, free lives, and an all-inclusive patriotism.
But he saw too clearly the disadvantages, as well as
the advantages, of each to be an enthusiastic partisan
or apostle of either by itself. He evidently saw that
cultured, Hellenic life could not be carried on without
the city-state (πόλις), and he could not help seeing that
such states were entirely unable to maintain themselves,
either against each other or against foreign aggression,
unless they were united and held together by a power
which they themselves could not create, and which
therefore had to come to them from without. Such a
power he looked for in some great hero, like Philip or
Alexander, who, standing among men like a god above
all institutions and laws, should govern them by divine
right. But as the divine man is rare,† and can not be
commanded, ordinary men must be content to make
and obey laws, the best they can evolve or secure.
Accordingly, in attempting to describe the highest
state which he conceives to be realizable without the
aid of the divine man (who is beyond science as beyond

* *Pol.*, iii, 13, 1283a 3 *sqq.*

† Σπάνιον τὸ θεῖον ἄνδρα εἶναι, *Eth. Nic.*, vii, 1, 1145a 27 *sq.*

12

law), he keeps pretty close to the model of the Greek city-state, merely suggesting such improvements upon actual conditions as shall make that institution truly and consciously a school of virtue.

In examining Aristotle's political scheme, we become aware of two characteristics of the man—(1) his extreme regard for facts and actual conditions, and (2) his lack of that prophetic vision which, amid the chaos and confusion of a transition period, can descry

> " The Spirit of the years to come
> Yearning to mix himself with Life."

The former of these made him not only accept many current notions and practices which were soon to be outgrown, but even to champion them as founded in Nature, and to seek a philosophical explanation of them. Thus, for example, he became an advocate of chattel slavery (although, as he himself tells us, there were already in his time men who held it to be unnatural *), of abortion, of the murder of feeble or deformed children, of the treatment of " barbarians " as generically inferior to Greeks, and fit only to be their slaves, of the exclusion of the industrial classes, as incapable of virtue, from all political power, etc. The second characteristic made him in great measure blind to those subtle humanitarian forces that were at work around him, slowly undermining the walls of Greek exclusiveness, and making straight the paths for him who was to know neither Greek nor barbarian, but only man. Hence it was that, though he could not help seeing that something like the œcumenic empire of Alexander must be the determining influ-

---

* Τοῖς δὲ (δοκεῖ) παρὰ φύσιν τὸ δεσπόζειν, *Pol.*, i, 3, 1253b 12.

ence in all future social life,* he could not in the least
forecast the broadening, humanizing influences of such
an institution. In fact, as has been recently pointed
out in a work referred to in a former chapter, Aristotle
was not a religious nature,† and accordingly he had
none of that large, vision-giving sympathy which usually goes with such natures, and none of that humility
in the presence of infinite perfection and an infinite
task which makes the differences between man and
man seem trifling and embraces all that is human in a
consciousness of universal brotherhood. Like his master Plato, and like the Greeks generally, he placed the
supreme happiness and end of man in an activity of
the intellect, without, however, including in it, as Plato
did, the element of love. This activity, which he
termed θεωρία—that is, vision of the divine (see p. 134,
note)—is not only a purely individual matter, but it is
an end which only a very small and select portion of

---

* There is a curious remark in the fourth book of the *Physics*,
where, speaking of the different senses in which one thing may
be *in* another, he includes among these the sense "in which the
affairs of the Greeks are in a king, and generally in the first motive" (power)—ὡς ἐν βασιλεῖ τὰ τῶν Ἑλλήνων καὶ ὅλως ἐν τῷ πρώτῳ
κινητικῷ, *Phys.*, iv, 3, 210a 21 *sq.* John Philoponus, in his commentary, explains this to mean that "the ruler is the creative
cause (ποιητικὸν αἴτιον) of political action " (πράγματα).

† Spicker, *Die Ursachen des Verfalls der Philosophie*, p. 120.
That the philosophy of Aristotle contributed much to Christian
theology since the fourth (see Harnack, *Dogmengeschichte*, iii, 8,
10), and particularly since the thirteenth, century, is most true;
but it is also true that its contributions did much to deface
the true character of the Christian religion (see Eucken, *Die
Philosophie des Thomas von Aquino und die Cultur der Neu-
zeit*, pp. 13 *sqq.* Cf. Green, *Prolegomena to Ethics*, pp. 274 *sqq.*).

humanity can ever hope to attain, and one that leaves no room for either love or will. That Aristotle should have set up this intellectual goal as the end of all human effort was due perhaps directly to the influence of Plato, and to his own doctrine that the end or happiness of every being consisted in the exercise of its highest or distinguishing faculty—in the case of man, reason ; but indirectly and originally in the generally growing conviction that the true life was diagogic and not practical, and that the highest *diagoge* was contemplation. Thus his supreme ideal grew out of the tendencies of his time, and not out of any deep religious consciousness.

Given a nature such as Aristotle's, one can almost forecast what his ethical and educational theory will be. His respect for the actual will induce him to give it a large influence in all his teachings, while his belief that man's supreme end is purely individual will make him set up the magnificent (μεγαλόψυχος), self-centered individuality as the ideal man. As he is destitute of the religious consciousness, his ethics will have no religious or divine sanction, but be purely experimental and prudential. In all this we can see clearly the struggle that was then going on between the claims of diagogic, and those of practical, life ; between the old ideal of small republics of equal freemen and the new reality of an empire governed by a magnificent personality standing above law ; and between the old personal gods of polytheism and the new impersonal, purely intelligent " Prime Mover," whose entire activity and life consist in thinking himself.

It would be surprising if Aristotle, or any man, writing in the midst of such struggles, whose issue still lay in the future, should have been able to draw up a perfectly consistent scheme of ethics and politics, at once keeping close to the actual, avoiding Platonic dreams, and yet bringing into consciousness the spirit of the time and its direction. Hence we need not be surprised to find that the *Ethics* and *Politics* not only contain glaring contradictions, but that they reveal nothing which could guide men out of the "dark forest" in which they found themselves. As scientific works they must ever hold a very high place on account of the immense mass of generalized knowledge which they present; but as offering any ultimate solution of ethical or political problems they are comparatively valueless. Upon the practical life of the centuries immediately following they exerted less influence than even the works of Plato, which, however fanciful, contained a definite enough ideal.

What, then, was the nature of the educational state which Aristotle attempted to construct on scientific principles, and what was the result of that attempt?

We may answer the former question by saying that Aristotle's educational state is little more than the Athenian democracy freed from abuses and excesses, and made a school of virtue. The education provided in it is simply the Athenian system improved, unified, and furnished with a definite end, lying within the scope of the state. It is unfortunate that we have only a fragment of Aristotle's scheme of education, and are therefore unable to say how he connected his political education with that which should prepare men for diagogic contemplation. As far as this fragment goes it deals solely with the education of the citizen, as citizen, of a small commonwealth.

By keeping close to the actual, Aristotle, no doubt, hoped that his scheme might be capable of realization; but the truth is it was as unrealizable as the *Republic* of Plato, and this for two reasons—(1) because the days of small independent republics were over, and an œcumenic state was about to take their place; and (2) because the moral forces which might have carried the reforms advocated by him did not exist, and he could show no way of bringing them into existence. It is easy, therefore, to answer the question, What was the result of his attempt to found a state on scientific principles? As far as the end contemplated was concerned, it was an absolute failure. Aristotle affected the world of his own time, not by propounding a political system, but by educating Alexander, who applied the only remedy which could do anything for the Greek republics—that of brute force. When, after Aristotle's death, his chief treatises (so the story goes) were hid away in a cellar in the Troad, from which they did not emerge for two hundred years, the world did not feel that it had lost anything, or move on otherwise than it would have done had they been in everybody's hands.

But, for all that, we should be greatly mistaken if we should conclude that Aristotle's works were written in vain, that they played no part in the world's history. Works like his are like seeds that take a long time to germinate, but which in the long run develop into larger and more enduring plants than those that are more hasty. Although, of the four great philosophic schools which flourished in the Hellenic world soon after the death of Aristotle, the Peripatetic seems to have been the least conspicuous, and to have attracted

the smallest number of disciples, it nevertheless lived
on with energy sufficient to keep alive the thought of
its founder until the day came when the world required it. It was natural enough that a philosophy
which called for research, experiment, broad knowledge, and sober thinking—a philosophy which tried to
make sure its footing upon the earth before it buried
its head in the clouds—should have proved less attractive than one which promised to raise men in the
luxurious chariot of imagination to the dreamy heaven
of pure ideas. But a philosophy based upon facts, if
it did not allure the many, could not at any time fail
to command the attention of serious thinkers really
desirous of arriving at the truth of the world, or in
the end to assert its natural right to cosmopolitanism.
For, however narrow Aristotle's political ideal may have
been, and however far behind the demands of the time,
his science and philosophy were in the highest degree
cosmopolitan. In this respect they stood alone and
without rivals. Hence, in proportion as the widening,
deepening, and complicating of human relations made
a cosmopolitan system of thought necessary, the philosophy of Aristotle inevitably came into the fore-
ground. It may be safely said that from his day to
ours no institution claiming to be cosmopolitan or
catholic has succeeded in establishing and maintaining itself without the aid of his thought, and that of
all the educational influences that have come to the
world from Greece that of Aristotle is the strongest.

In truth, Aristotle occupies a unique place in the
ancient world. He is the exponent of the thoughts
and tendencies which marked the epoch in which it
passed from ethnic to cosmopolitan life. He writes

the testament of the former, and in large degree the programme of the latter. With him the education of Greece comes to an end; she ceases to be a pupil and becomes a teacher. She leaves her little school, not without some bitter regrets and a few tears, and goes out into the wide world to conquer and instruct. Her history from that time on, in so far as it has any human interest, consists in what she did outside her own boundaries, in imparting her education and culture to the declining East and the rising West.

The important question that now presents itself to us is this: Wherein did Greek education and culture consist? It has been the aim of this and the previous chapters to supply the materials for an answer to this question, and it ought not now to be difficult to render. We may express it in a few words: Greek culture, the result of Greek education, consisted in elevating the individual from thraldom to the blind forces of Nature, whether in the form of religious superstition or social prescription, to a position of self-determination or moral freedom. We have tried to trace the course of this process. It may be here briefly recapitulated.

The Greeks, when we first meet with them in history, are living, like the rest of mankind, in societies held together by blood-ties, maintained by religious rites having their origin in these ties. In so far as a moral personality can be said to exist at all, it is the community—the family or the tribe—and not the individual, who indeed has no recognized existence except as a member of the community. The religion of this period is animism or ancestor-worship. In course of time, through migration and the union of families, the blood-tie gradually gives place to the land-tie, as the result of which the monogamic family begins to appear and claim a certain independence, which it is able to maintain by private property in land. The religion of this period is the worship of the powers of Nature—polytheism—which, however, only gradually and partially replaces ancestor-worship. After a time again, through the multiplication of families and the appropriation of all the available land by a certain number of them, leaving the rest landless, there grows up a distinction of classes, a distinction between gentle and simple. In order to protect their common interests against the others, the members of the landed class unite, build a common residence or stronghold (πόλις), eschew labor, establish a common worship, and begin city-life. The bond in this case is neither blood nor land, but worth (ἀρετή), and this is reflected in the new gods, who no longer represent natural powers, but spiritual powers. Though polytheism is not yet overcome, the way is paved for a spiritual monotheism. To bring this about only requires the growth of reflection. And this soon makes its appearance as the result of leisure.

Up to this point the history of all peoples seems to have been pretty much the same. But now two different lines of development are possible, and some peoples take the one, some the other. Some, like the Hebrews, whose reflection is of an ethical sort, push straight forward to monotheism and develop a truly spiritual religion. Others, in whom reflection takes a purely intellectual turn, gradually abandon the religious attitude altogether and tend to find a basis for practical life in metaphysical ideas. Among these must be counted the Greeks. When reflective thought first begins among them, it does, indeed, tend for a brief period to monotheism through a cosmogonic, and later through an ethical, interpretation of the old mythology;* but this tendency is soon abandoned and attention directed to physical nature, for whose phenomena an explanation is demanded in terms of itself—that is, of something physical. But as reflection proceeds, it learns that such an explanation involves an impossibility, and finds itself gradually forced to make metaphysical assumptions—such as atoms, ratio, mind. But these afford no moral sanction, and so, when the gods are replaced by impersonal metaphysical entities, the chief bond of society is broken and the individual man is declared to be the measure of all things. Inasmuch as all morality has thus far been social, and society has rested upon religion, the immediate result is moral confusion, for which the Sophists are in large degree responsible. Deplorable as this confusion may seem, when looked at from without, it is nevertheless only the first crude expression of man's earliest attempt at self-determination, and as such must be judged leniently. In fact, if we consider carefully and judge calmly, we shall have to admit that the Protagorean substitution of man for God as the universal determiner is the germ of that ferment which has resulted in the new wine of moral freedom. Man had to break away from the old gods, whose rule annulled human freedom, and find new gods, or, more truly, a new God, whose rule was compatible with it. The latter was the

---

* The former we find in the so-called Orphic poetry and in the fragments of Pherecydes (which may contain Semitic elements), the latter in the plays of Æschylus.

task which Socrates set himself, and which, indeed, he accomplished, by discovering in man a universal divine element, which indeed *is* the measure of all things. This was the greatest discovery ever made by any human being, and the one that renders possible moral life, whether individual, social, or political. But there still remained the question: How shall this discovery be made the principle of social life? To the task of answering this, first Plato and then Aristotle addressed themselves. But the former misstated the question in asking it, and then allowed his judgment to be warped by personal and class prejudices, while the latter, though he put the question correctly, lacked a clear consciousness of that divine element which alone could have enabled him to give the correct answer. Thus both equally failed to discover the concrete social embodiment of moral freedom, leaving to the world only cunningly constructed schemes incapable of realization. This was the condition of things when Aristotle died, and the education of Greece as a nation came to a close. The task of the Greek people had not been accomplished; but it had risen into clear consciousness and become an object of serious effort.

As might have been expected, a problem originally set by actual life was solved, not in the field of speculation, but in that of practice, under the pressure of social and individual needs. What Aristotle failed to do his pupil Alexander went far to accomplish. By breaking down and absorbing in his empire the little Greek states in which the individual had previously found his spiritual solidarity or sphere of ethical action, he compelled him to look for this solidarity elsewhere. The immediate result was the formation of private

societies, or philosophic schools, whose members were
bound together by a common system of truth, in accordance with which they sought to shape their individual lives. These societies were entirely disconnected
with the state and admitted to their membership persons of all nations, tongues, and classes. Here, therefore, for the first time in history we find men united
by the universal divine element in them, and, under
the influence of this, setting at naught all other bonds,
whether of family, race, or religion. Here for the first
time we find cosmopolitanism and a sense of the spiritual solidarity of humanity.

I am strongly of the belief that the part played by
the Greek philosophic schools in cherishing this sense,
and so paving the way for a universal moral institution, has never been sufficiently recognized. Still it
was not in the schools founded by Plato and Aristotle
that this work was most effectively done, but in two
others that arose soon after the death of the latter—
the Stoic and the Epicurean, and especially in the
former. The brilliant intellectual results attained by
Plato and Aristotle have in great measure blinded us
to the far more important moral results accomplished
by the schools of Zeno and Epicurus. Moreover, the
work of these latter was in time completely thrown
into shadow by the far more splendid work of the
" divine man " of Nazareth, while that of the other
two remained without a peer. In spite of this, if we
would understand the last stages in the process by
which the task of the Greeks was accomplished and
moral liberty made the principle of human life, we
must consider and try to understand the work done
by the Stoics and Epicureans. In this connection it

is, of course, their practical tenets rather than their metaphysical principles that interest us; but, inasmuch as the former necessarily depend in some degree on the latter, we must cast a glimpse at these also.

Wide as the two systems in question stand apart, their fundamental positions differ only in this respect, that the one is founded upon intellect and the other upon sense. This, indeed, is a wide enough difference, and all their separate peculiarities follow from it. Both are equally materialistic; but while Stoicism, drawing upon the thought of Heraclitus, holds matter to be a *continuum*, moved and governed by an inherent, all-pervading reason (λόγος), Epicureanism, inspired by Democritus, regards it as composed of atoms individually moved by a blind impulse. Both subordinate the theoretical to the practical, and tend to take the place of religion. From the monism of Stoicism there follow two conclusions bearing closely upon ethics— (1) that the universe is governed by necessity or fate, (2) that man is an integral part of the universe so governed, and therefore has no free will. Thus, under the influence of materialism, the Socratic doctrine that men are one through a common divine, freeing element in them turns over into the doctrine that the divine alone has any real existence, and that men are mere temporary manifestations of it. It may seem strange that, with a belief like this, there should be room in Stoicism for any ethical system at all; but the fact is, it comprises a higher and more complete ethical system than ever had been known before. To Stoicism we owe the conception and first name of duty (καθῆκον), the notion of complete personal independence, and the ideal of universal brotherhood, three of the chief forces that have shaped, and are shaping, modern civilization. No doubt, its notions of duty and personal independence were exaggerated and at bottom false; but their very exaggeration did much to impress them for all time upon the world. We can easily forgive the rigorous discipline by which the Stoic strove to make himself the organ of the universal Logos, in defiance of all the demands of sense, as well as his self-sufficiency when he thought he had succeeded, when we remember that the same pantheistic doctrine which resulted in these also took the form of a vigorous universal human sympathy such as we should vainly look for in pre-Stoic times.* If theoretically the Stoics were governed by reason, in their practical relations with men they were governed by sympathy, which is the first step toward love.

Of all the philosophic systems of the ancient world Stoicism was, morally speaking, the highest and produced the noblest men—Marcus Aurelius, Epictetus, Seneca, etc.—and nothing prevented it from being the true and ultimate concrete form of moral life but its metaphysical basis, its materialism, fatalism, and practical atheism. As a system of ethics divorced from religion, it is unsurpassed and unsurpassable; but as a solution of the problem of moral life in the deepest sense, in the sense of a free life in a world of free personalities, it is necessarily a failure.

We can afford to pass by Epicureanism with very slight notice for two reasons—(1) because it added no

---

* There is, indeed, a dawning of it in the Æschylean Prometheus, who in very many respects was a Stoic before Stoicism. The word "philanthropic" ($\phi\iota\lambda\acute{\alpha}\nu\theta\rho\omega\pi\sigma$) occurs first in the *Prom.*, lines 11, 28.

new element to Greek education, and (2) because, notwithstanding its long history of six hundred years, it contributed no element to cosmopolitan life. It is essentially materialistic, sensual, hedonistic, and atheistic, and is rather a system of ethical despair than of ethics. Curiously enough, in strong contrast to Stoicism, it champions and emphasizes the freedom of the will. The bond of union among Epicureans was friendship, the most subjective of all relations, as Erdmann says. In adopting this they returned to Aristotelianism and fell short of the Stoic universal sympathy.

Four distinguished men undertook to solve the problem propounded by Socrates: How can the universal divine principle in man be made the basis of a concrete social moral life?—two of them, Plato and Aristotle, theoretically, and two, Zeno and Epicurus, practically. All failed, each for a different reason. With their attempts were exhausted the possibilities of solution with the resources of Greek thought and life alone. Just as all attempts to found a united Greek empire by means of internal forces failed, and success was reserved for a foreign conqueror, so all attempts to solve the problem which the unfolding of Greek life and thought propounded failed as long as only internal resources alone were drawn upon. Greece had to go beyond herself to solve her own riddle.

We, looking back from a distance of two thousand years, can easily see where the difficulty lay, and can not but wonder that a solution which looks as if it must have lain before the feet of everybody should have been obstinately disregarded. But our wonder will cease when we remember how persistent and how blinding are philosophical prepossessions, especially when they have passed through a number of phases. Just as the Lockean dogma that all knowledge comes through the five senses has, in one form or another, become a blinding prepossession of modern thought, preventing it from seeing the most obvious solutions of many vexed problems of philosophy and practice, so the Platonic conception of God as an abstract idea became an unreasoned presupposition of all subsequent Greek thought, closing its eyes to the only truth which was needed for the solution of its supreme question. Before the Greek mind can advance further, it must absorb a foreign element, and to a consideration of this we must next address ourselves.

CHAPTER VIII.

IT is often said that a good teacher learns as much from his pupils as they do from him. This was exemplified in the case of the Greeks when they became masters of the East and undertook to impart their culture to it. While Greece in her little polities was working out her new civilization, she had suffered grievously at the hands of the older civilizations of the East. When at last, united by a foreign conqueror and made a province of his empire, she was placed in a commanding position with respect to the other provinces, she began the spiritual conquest of her old foe— the Hellenization of the East. It is true that, long before the advent of Alexander, there had been a very extensive Greek *Diaspora*, carrying Greek ideas and practices into many parts of the East; but, like the Jewish *Diaspora*, it had earned little respect and exerted comparatively little influence. It was only when Greeks and their culture were placed in a position where they could not be disregarded or contemned that they began to exercise an all-transforming influence. Then, however, the process went on rapidly. Within a century after Alexander's death the whole of the then known East was saturated with Greek ideas and habits.

13

Even the conservative Palestinian Jews were so deeply affected by them that even the great and glorious Maccabæan reaction in favor of pure Jehovistic religion and theocracy did not suffice to eradicate them completely.*

At first, of course, the results of Greek teaching showed themselves in externals—in the establishment of Greek schools, palæstras, gymnasia, theatres, and stadia; but it was not long before the deeper elements of Greek culture—art and philosophy, especially the latter—began to find a fruitful soil among the " barbarians." Indeed, it is a remarkable and somewhat inexplicable fact that nearly all the great names in Greek philosophy after the death of Aristotle are names not of Greeks, but of Orientals. Even the founder of Stoicism, Zeno, seems to have been a Phœnician, or perhaps a Hittite. But, however much the Orientals might wish to adopt the victorious and fashionable Hellenism, they came to Greek thought with Oriental temperaments and Oriental prepossessions. While, therefore, the philosophy which they professed might call itself Greek, and in its outward form really was so, it contained inner or material elements which were not Greek, and which deeply affected even those which were.

These elements were, on the whole, of a religious sort, so that from the time when Greek thought came in contact with the East it began to be religious. Naturally it was only religious conceptions of a high order, such as were capable of philosophic expression, that

---

* This influence may be traced in *Ecclesiastes*, and is prominent in the *Apocrypha*. See Schürer, *History of the Jews in the Time of Christ*, *passim*.

were able to coalesce with Greek thought. Among
such conceptions there were four that specially characterized the higher religions of the East: (1) that of
the personality and transcendence of God; (2) that of
inferior divinities, standing in the relation of ministers
to the supreme God; (3) that of a past revelation of
the divine will to or in man through these ministers;
(4) that of a future revealer. These conceptions are
common to the two higher Oriental religions with
which we are best acquainted, and whose canonical
literature, in part at least, remains to us—Zoroastrianism and Judaism.

In Zoroastrianism we find a god who, if not actually supreme, is at least potentially so, since his ultimate victory is assured—Ahura Mazda, the personal
and transcendent "creator of earth, water, trees,
mountains, roads, wind, sleep, and light," and "father
of the six Amesha Spentas, the father of all gods." *
Subordinate to him are a large number of divine beings, the highest of whom are the Amesha Spentas,
originally abstract attributes of the supreme deity,
afterward hypostasized into angelic personalities.†
Through these beings Ahura Mazda communicates
his will to man either by inspiration or by incarnation. The oldest documents of the Zoroastrian religion, the Gâthas, are full of supplications for divine
inspiration,‡ and there can be little doubt that Zoro-

---

* Darmesteter, translation of the *Zend-Avesta*, Introduction,
p. lxi.

† *Ibid.*, p. lix *sqq.* Mills' translation of the *Zend-Avesta*,
Introduction, p. xxiv; cf. Cheyne, *The Origin and Religious
Contents of the Psalter*, p. 334.

‡ " The wonderful idea that God's attributes are his messen-

aster himself was regarded as the incarnation of a divine spirit. * Lastly, Zoroastrianism looks forward to a Savior, Saoshyant, who will spring from the seed of Zoroaster, and who, by finally overcoming Angro Mainyus, will introduce the eternal age of bliss.†

If we turn to Judaism, we find essentially the same fundamental conceptions, with merely Semitic and national limitations. At the summit of existence is one God, the creator of heaven and earth. Subordinate to him are the angels, otherwise called sons of God,‡ holy ones, # etc. That these were originally mere attributes or aspects of God, gradually distinguished from him and personified, is clear enough from many passages of the Hebrew Scriptures,‖ and was observed by Philo.ᐃ Through these God communicates his will

---

gers sent out into the human soul to ennoble and redeem makes him (Zoroaster) at times so subtle that the latest scholars can not tell whether he means Asha and Vohu Manah personified as archangels, or as the thoughts and beneficent intentions of the Deity reproduced in man."—Mills' *Zend-Avesta*, Introduction, p. xxiv.

* "All the features in Zarathustra point to a god."—Darmesteter, Introduction to *Zend-Avesta*, p. lxxix; cf. *Farvardên Yast*, cap. xxiv.

† "A maid bathing in the Lake Kāsava will conceive by it (the seed of Zoroaster), and bring forth the victorious Saoshyant, who will come from the region of the dawn, to free the world from death and decay, from corruption and rottenness, ever living and ever thriving, when the dead shall arise and immortality commence."—Darmesteter, *ut sup.* Cf. *Zamyâd Yast*, cap. xv.

‡ Job, ii, 1; xxxviii, 7; Psalms, xxix, 1; lxxxix, 7; Dan. iii, 25, etc.

Job, v, 1; xv, 15; Psalms, lxxxix, 6, 7.

‖ Gen. i, 26; xviii, 1–3; xxxii, 24–31; Job, ii, 1, etc.

ᐃ See Drummond, *Philo Judæus*, vol. ii, book iii, chap. v.

to men, and, indeed, governs the world.* And, lastly,
the Jewish belief in a coming Messiah is too well
known to require more than a passing remark.

Such, then, were the four leading characteristics of
the two great and widely spread religions with which
Greek thought came in close contact after the conquest
of Alexander. While it might, and, on the whole,
did, ignore such inferior religions as the Babylonian,
Egyptian, and Phœnician, it could not disregard these
or remain unaffected by them, especially as in some of
their characteristics they supplied its most marked
deficiencies, and gave life and concreteness to some of
its dead, abstract conceptions. To the Greek, God was
an abstraction—the Good, Intelligence, or the like;
his agents, whereby he acted upon the world, were
numbers, ratios, or ideas; the revelation of him was a
mere intellectual vision of these; what hope there was
of anything better in the future was confined to a wish
and a vague hope that a "divine man" † might some
day appear. To the Persian and the Jew, on the contrary, God was a living, holy, all-knowing, all-powerful
personality, searching the hearts and trying the reins
of every human being, in whose sight the heavens were
not clean, and who charged his angels with folly; his
agents were living persons—his sons, holy ones—doing his holy will with obedient might; the revelation

---

* See the argument in the first chapter of the *Epistle to the
Hebrews*, and compare Everling, *Die paulinische Angelologie
und Dæmonologie, passim.*

† See Æschylus, *Prom. Vinct.*, 844 *sqq.*; Aristotle, *Politics*,
iii, 13 ; 1284a 3 *sqq.*; *Eth. Nic.*, vii, 1 ; 1145a 15 *sqq.*; Plato, *Phœdo*,
85 D. (where a "Divine Word," θεῖος λόγος, is looked forward to
as a possibility).

of him was a manifestation of that holy will to chosen
lawgivers (Moses, Zoroaster), in the form of a law determining conduct, and promising the favor of Him in
whose hands are life and death ; the hope of the future
centered upon the certain appearance of a great divine
person, who should put an end to evil, consign its
agents to everlasting darkness, and usher in for the
good an eternity of holiness and happiness, in the presence and service of the Lord of the Universe.

That Greek thinkers should remain indifferent to
such conceptions as these, or that Orientals, on becoming acquainted with Greek philosophy, should abandon
them, would have been strange indeed. On the one
hand, they were just what that philosophy needed in
order to give its principles life, reality, and motive
power; and, on the other, philosophy was what they
needed in order to give them a universal and rational
expression. We need not be surprised, therefore, to
find that, under the rule of Alexander's successors,
Greek philosophy begins to borrow theological beliefs
from Zoroastrianism and Judaism, while these religions
begin to express their beliefs in philosophic form. The
former tendency shows itself in all the schools of Greek
thought soon after they are transplanted to Alexandria;
the latter, in the rise of Perso-Hellenic and Judæo-
Hellenic religious philosophies, based upon sacred writings. After a time the results of these two tendencies
united, thenceforth to flow on in a single stream.

The truth is, in the process whereby Hellenic genius
continued its mission through union with Orientalism
we must distinguish two stages. In the former of
these, while Hellenism borrows from Orientalism, and
Orientalism from Hellenism, each maintains a distinct

existence and stands consciously opposed to the other, Hellenism being prevailingly philosophic and natural-istic, Orientalism prevailingly religious and spiritual-istic. In the latter, the opposition between the two ceases; philosophy and religion, nature and spirit, are co-ordinated. The abstract ideas and relations of phi-losophy are identified with the gods and angels of re-ligion; the process of the world becomes the expression of the divine reason (λόγος). It is only in this second stage that Greek thought really finds its completion.

Since the days of the Renaissance it has been usual to regard this union of Hellenism and Orientalism as a corruption and a degradation, as a mingling of clear thought with superstition, as the end of science and the source of delusion. The larger historic outlook of the present day is teaching us to draw a very different conclusion, and to see in the four world-transform-ing results of this union—Christianity, Neoplatonism, Manichæism, and Mohammedanism—a growth and a consummation. The strongest of the four is that in which the union is most complete.

It is not easy, for want of documents, to follow the process of the gradual infiltration of Oriental concep-tions into Greek philosophy, and Zeller has done his best to ignore their influence. Nevertheless, the re-sults that ultimately followed in the forms of Neo-pythagoreanism and Neoplatonism leave no doubt that it was real and pervasive. Epicureanism, as being least of a philosophy and hostile to religion, was but little affected; but Platonism, Aristotelianism, and Stoicism underwent considerable changes, which had the effect of partially obliterating their differences and bringing them together. And there was a fifth philosophy, which, after having long smoldered in obscurity, now came again to the surface, and proved more able and ready than all the rest to marry with Orientalism. This was Pythagoreanism. This remarkable and still imperfectly understood system had, on account of its social and antipolitical—we might almost say, its ecclesiastical—tendencies, been suppressed in its institutional form in the region of its birth, Magna Græcia, in the fifth century B. C. In spite of this its principles had lived on, cherished by a few select and strongly religious spirits, and from time to time making its presence felt in other systems, notably in that of Plato. Now, at last, when the small Greek states, which had found its influence disorganizing, were placed in a position of subordination to a higher power, which could permit freedom of thought and freedom of organization, it came forth from its concealment and claimed a leading place in the world of thought, a place which it soon conquered for itself.*

Though each of these philosophies long maintained a separate existence and a separate school, yet, thanks partly to the new political conditions, partly to the influence of Oriental religions, there were many important points and tendencies in which the four last-named agreed. To the former cause were due the separation of ethics from politics, the tendency to cosmopolitanism or humanitarianism, and the effect of men to withdraw from the business and interests of the world and to find their happiness in states of their

---

* The history of Pythagoreanism has still to be written. Röth's account is uncritical, Zeller's hypercritical and tendentious.

own consciousness, in some form of restful self-possession. To the latter were due the connection of
ethics with theology or religion, the separation of religion from statecraft, and the extreme importance
assigned to it. All these common characteristics might
be summed up in one—a tendency to religious, as distinct from political, life. This, indeed, is the common
mark of all post-Aristotelian thought. But, although
philosophy thus became religious, and did so largely
under Oriental influence, it was long before it adopted
any one of the four leading tenets that marked the
higher religions of the East. What Orientalism at
first did for Greek thought was not to impart to it
new tenets, but to give it a new direction, and a new,
a religious consecration. Later it was otherwise.

It need hardly be said that it was Zoroastrianism,
and not Judaism, that affected Greek thought in the
age immediately succeeding Aristotle. There is no
sufficient proof that Aristotle knew anything of the
Jewish faith, whereas the religion of Zoroaster was
known to the Greeks long before, probably as early as
the time of Pythagoras. Democritus is said to have
visited Persia, and Herodotus, though he does not
mention Zoroaster, refers to many traits of his religion
(i, 131–140). Plato mentions him by name, and calls
him the son of Ahura Mazda ('Ωρομάζης).* Aristotle
is said to have written a book on Magianism (Μαγικός),

---

* *Alcibiad.*, i, 122 A. The authenticity of this dialogue is
doubtful. See Zeller, *Philos. der Griech.*, ii, 418, and cf. Her-
mann, *Gesch. und System der plat. Philos.*, p. 439 *sqq.* Clem-
ens Alexandrinus (*Strom.*, v. p. 711) identifies Er, the Pamphyl-
ian, whose wonderful story is told in the tenth book of the
Republic, with Zoroaster !

and, though this is doubtful, it is certain that he was acquainted with Magian thought,* and considered the Magian religion older than the Egyptian.† From this time on the Magian system seems to have been quite familiar to the Greek world.‡ Indeed, one element of it—viz., Magian divination—seems to have been familiar to it much earlier. Aristotle is quoted as authority for the statement that a Magian from Syria prophesied to Socrates the whole course of his life and his violent death.* Be this as it may, there seems little doubt that certain leading characteristics of Hellenistic philosophic religion, its mysticism, its theurgy, its divination, etc., were largely due to Zoroastrian influence. It is well known that about the Christian era the worship of Mithras prevailed nearly all over the Roman Empire, and that it was for centuries a powerful rival to Christianity, which apparently borrowed some features from it.‖

With regard to the influence of Judaism upon Greek philosophy we are better informed. This influence must have begun about the middle of the third century B. C., when the Hebrew Scriptures were translated into Greek. It soon grew so powerful that many

---

* *Metaph.*, iv, 4, 1091b, 10. Here we are told that "the Magians consider the first begetter (creator?) the Supreme Being."

† Dialogue Περὶ Φιλοσοφίας, frag. 8. He adds, "And according to them (the Magi) there are two first principles—a good power and an evil power (δαίμων), the name of the former being Zeus and Oromasdes, that of the latter Hades and Areimanios.

‡ See Windischmann, *Zoroastrische Studien*, pp. 260–313.

* Diog. Laert., *Life of Socrates*, xxiv, 45.

‖ See Harnack, *Dogmengeschichte*, vol. i, pp. 105, 395.

Greeks became proselytes to Judaism and many more sincere admirers of its principles. It formed a powerful element in Neopythagoreanism, and greatly helped to encourage a belief in prophesy and direct divine revelations.*

When we come to consider the effect of Hellenic thought on the two great religions of the East—Zoroastrianism and Judaism—we have to confess that our knowledge of its effect on the former is very meagre indeed. The reason of this is that Zoroastrianism practically disappeared from the world twelve hundred years ago, and that the records of its attempts to find an expression in philosophy mostly perished with it. But that the Zoroastrians tried to combine their religion with Greek thought there can be no doubt; and some of the results of this combination were far-reaching indeed, contributing elements to Neoplatonism, Christian Gnosticism, Manichæism, Mohammedanism, and Mysticism. That the Magians had a sort of philosophic theology even before they became acquainted with the Greeks seems clear from the statement of Aristotle quoted on p. 186, as well as from the esteem which their sages generally enjoyed. Indeed, even the most ancient form of Zoroastrianism with which we are acquainted, that which appears in the Gâthas, is already a philosophy of a high order, albeit it is not expressed in strictly philosophical language. But shortly after the time of Alexander, who, it may be remarked, is said to have destroyed a large portion of the sacred books of the Zoroastrians, a distinct change takes place in the Persian religion, what we

---

* See Zeller, *Philos. der Griechen*, v, 62 *sq.* (2d edit.).

might call a tendency to rationalism.   Whereas in the Gâthas, which, I believe, are the only part of the Zend-Avesta that fairly represent the religion of the Magi before Alexander, the supreme powers are the strongly personal Ahura Mazda and Angro Mainyus, in the later parts of that work we find the beginning of a tendency to personify certain abstractions and elevate them to the highest place, a tendency which afterward became very pronounced.   " When the Magi had accounted for the existence of evil by the existence of two principles, there arose the question how there could be two principles, and a longing for unity was felt, which found its satisfaction in the assumption that both are derived from one and the same principle.   This principle was, according to divers sects, either Space, or Infinite Light, or Boundless Time, or Fate.   Of most of these systems no direct trace is found in the Avesta, yet they existed already in the time of Aristotle." *   Spiegel, in his *Erânische Alterthumskunde* (vol. ii, pp. 4–19), treats these and several other principles as " extramundane deities," admitting that they are not prominent in the *Zend-Avesta ;* but the truth is they bear the same relation to the true divinities of Zoroastrianism that the abstract principles of the Greek philosophers—number, ratio, love, hate,

---

* Darmesteter, *Zend-Avesta*, Introd., p. lxxxii.   In a note reference is made to a passage from Eudemus, the pupil of Aristotle, in which he says: " As to the Magi, and the whole Arian stock, some of them call the whole Intelligible and Unified Space, others call it Time, holding that out of this are distinguished a good God and an evil Power, and that light and darkness are prior to these, as some maintain."—Wolf's *Anecdota Græca*, vol. iii, p. 259.

intellect, being, necessity, etc.—bear to the gods of Greece. How far they are due to Greek influence is at present uncertain; but to some extent they certainly are so.

In dealing with this question we must carefully distinguish between the Zoroastrianism of Persia and that of the Persian *Diaspora*.* The former, coming but slightly in contact with Greek influences, was naturally but little affected by them, whereas the latter seems to have been greatly modified. One of the most conspicuous results of this modification was the rise of the worship of Mithras, which in the *Diaspora* seem almost to have superseded that of Ahura Mazda. Indeed, the worship of Mithras bore very much the same relation to Zoroastrianism that Christianity, later on, did to Judaism.

Far more than Zoroastrianism, Judaism was influenced by Greek thought. This influence is already faintly manifested in the book of *Ecclesiastes*, and is unmistakable in the *Septuagint*, which belongs in the main to the third century B. C. It went on increasing until it culminated in systematic attempts to read the whole of Greek philosophy into the Law and the Prophets of the Old Testament. Of these attempts the most successful, most far-reaching, and best known is that of Philo Judæus (B. C. 20 to A. D. 70), whose works are to a large extent still extant. This profoundly religious and subtle writer tried to interpret the Pentateuch in terms of the thought of Plato and

---

* There was a large Zoroastrian population in Armenia, Cappadocia, Syria, and other parts of western Asia. Herodotus (i, 135) says, "The Persians adopt foreign customs (νόμαια) more readily than any other people."

Zeno,* and thereby to elevate Judaism to the position of a universal religion.

The part which Philo played in combining the highest form of Orientalism with Greek thought is so important that we must devote a little space to him. Until recently it was usual to speak of Philo with a sort of kindly contempt, as merely an ancient Swedenborg, as a dreamer who tried to persuade himself that all Greek philosophy had been borrowed from Moses, and might be found in his writings by any one who had acquired the secret of interpreting them, the gist of the secret being that they were allegories. While there is truth in this, it is not the whole truth. The reason why Philo tried to combine Greek thought with Hebrew religion was that he had attained an insight, such as no man before him had possessed, into what was the deepest need of his day. He saw that an œcumenic empire needed an œcumenic religion, and since no such religion seemed to be forthcoming, he undertook to present the scheme of one.† Like the pious Jew he was, he believed that his religion, as having alone come from God, could alone hope to become universal. But as he could not help seeing that it was not universal, the question arose how it could be made so. His answer was, By being thrown into a

---

* See Drummond, *Philo Judæus, or The Jewish-Alexandrian Philosophy in its Development and Completion,* and cf. Bruno Bauer, *Philo, Strauss und Renan und das Urchristenthum* (Berlin, 1874).

† Nothing shows more clearly the essentially religious character of the ancient state and the difficulty of finding a suitable religion for the œcumenic empire than the claim to divinity advanced by the Roman emperors.

form of truth which is universal. Now, the only universal-seeming form of truth with which he was acquainted was that eclectic form of Greek philosophy which had resulted from the gradual convergence of Platonic, Aristotelian, and Stoic conceptions. The conclusion was obvious: Judaism, in order to become the universal religion, must be expressed in this eclectic philosophy. A little consideration showed further that this could be accomplished only if the records of the Hebrew religion were treated as allegories, whose true meaning could be drawn out only by philosophical interpretation. And so Philo treats them. We may blame this method as much as we please—and it is a false method, which science must forever disown—nevertheless we shall be constrained to admit two things: (1) that he rarely allowed it to draw him away from the truth; and (2) that he succeeded in outlining a religion which we are tempted to say was worthy to be universal.*

If we ask ourselves why it did not become so, we shall find that the reasons were, in the main, two: (1) Philo, with all his breadth and spirituality, was entirely unable to break down in his own mind the wall that separated Jew from Gentile, and made the former a privileged being; (2) with all his love and admiration for the Jewish Jehovah, he allowed Greek philosophy to transform this living God, this personal sustainer of moral life, into a mere abstraction, nay, the emptiest of all abstractions—Being. Thus, not-

---

* See, in the work of Bruno Bauer above referred to (p. 190, note), the chapters, *Philo as Guide from Hellenism to Christianity* (i), and *Philo's Spiritual World-Religion.* Cf. Bigg, *The Christian Platonists of Alexandria*, Lecture I.

withstanding much that is noble in Philo's system, these two defects proved fatal to its claim to be the world-religion. The supplement which Greek thought required in order to make the moral principle of Socrates the form of social life it did not find in Philo. It had to look further.

When Philo had drawn up his religious scheme, there were in the Hellenic world three movements, each endeavoring more or less blindly to shape itself into the universal religion which was felt to be the need of the time, that for want of which the souls of men were dying. The first was eclectic Greek philosophy, in the main a compound of Platonism, Aristotelianism, and Stoicism, with certain tendencies borrowed from Zoroastrianism and Judaism. The second was Hellenized Zoroastrianism, a system in which the old Mazdean personal powers of Good and Evil had been replaced by material abstractions—Time, Space, Light, Darkness—and whose religious service consisted of mysterious, material, theurgic rites, performed chiefly to Mithras, who was frequently identified with the Sun.* The third was Hellenized Judaism, or, as it is often called, Philonism, a system which, in attempting to ingraft the personal moral God of Moses and the Prophets upon the best thought of Greece, had allowed that God to renounce that which gave him his supreme worth—his moral personality—and sink down into the emptiest of metaphysical inanities. All these

---

* This curious compound has never, so far as I know, been fully investigated, or its effects upon subsequent thought and practice carefully traced. It seems to me to have contained many Stoic conceptions, and to have played a greater part in the growth of Christian thought than is generally admitted.

three systems were aiming at the same thing, viz., peace and rest for the soul, which, with the breaking down of the old polities, had lost its moorings and was tossed upon a tempestuous, seemingly boundless, shoreless sea. All three failed in their quest, for two reasons: (1) because they did not understand wherein peace of soul consists, (2) because they failed to discover the essential condition of such peace. All three conceived peace of soul to consist of two elements: (1) apathy with respect to the facts of the real world, (2) an intellectual or material union with the supreme abstraction. All were ascetic and world-renouncing opiates for euthanasia, not stimulants to life. As might have been expected, eclectic Hellenism occupied a middle ground between the extreme materialism of Hellenized Zoroastrianism and the extreme idealism of Philonism.*

With the failure of these movements, it seems as if Greek thought were never to accomplish its task of elevating man to concrete moral freedom, as if the education of the Greek people had been in vain. But Philo was still in all the vigor of manhood, when, in an obscure corner of the fatherland of his people, there arose a man who, without any parade of philosophic

---

* It need hardly be remarked that there were other compounds of Hellenism and Judaism besides Philonism. What Philonism was to the *diaspora*, Essenism was to native Judaism. Essenism, if we may believe two such scholars as Zeller (*Philosophie der Griechen*, vol. v, p. 279 *sqq.*) and Schürer (*Geschichte des jüd. Volkes*), was a compound of Judaism and Pythagoreanism. I can not but think, with Hilgenfeld, that it contained Zoroastrian elements—for example, a very pronounced dualism.

14

acquirement,* gave to the world in the simplest, most practical way that for which philosophy had searched in vain. We shall not, I think, misrepresent the teaching of Jesus if we say that it consisted in showing (1) what true peace of soul is, (2) what is the essential condition of that peace. He said : The soul finds peace only in love, such as takes the form of beneficent action toward one's fellows ; and the condition of such human love is divine love, taking the form of obedience to the mystic voice uttering itself in the soul and claiming authority, as coming from the Supreme Personality which is the condition of our being.

If we consider for a moment this teaching, we shall see (1) that it not only accords with the fundamental principles of moral freedom enunciated by Socrates, but that it lifts that principle out of abstractness into concreteness, giving its empty form an all-sufficient content ; (2) that it thus supplies the very element for which all the philosophies of the time had been searching in vain, a practical and realizable form of life capable of being developed into an œcumenic social order; and (3) that it throws back the light of a universal meaning and purpose upon the whole course of Greek education, which but for it would have ended in superstition, skepticism, or despair. If, moreover, reverting to the first of these points, we ask whence the Nazarene derived that content with which he filled the abstract form of Socrates, we shall find that it came from the exercise of a faculty which Socrates had been dimly conscious of in himself, but whose nature and object

---

† There seems no good reason for assuming that Jesus was unacquainted with the philosophic and religious movements of his time.

he had never brought into clearness—the sense of the
supernatural and eternal. He had felt in his soul the
presence of something divine (δαιμόνιόν τι), guiding him
to a goal higher than any that he could see, and he had
piously followed it with humble faith; but his dim,
confused Hellenic conceptions of the divine nature
had prevented him from seeing its true meaning.
Jesus not only felt the same thing in a far higher
degree, but with his lofty Hebrew conception of God
he was enabled to interpret his feeling, and say, I and
the Father are one. In this way he rose to the clear
consciousness of a personal God, the unity and spring
of that universal reason in which all mankind are one,
and through which alone they can enter into a free
corporate union. The followers of Socrates, even Plato
and Aristotle, had almost completely failed to catch
the meaning and bearing of Socrates's " dæmon," or
faculty of direct divine experience, and had tried to
reach the divine by a mere dialectic process. As a
result they reached only a bald abstraction—the Good,
the Prime Movent—which they vainly tried to substitute for the living God of actual experience. The immediate followers of Jesus being, like himself, trained *
in Judaism, were more fortunate. Instead of substituting dialectic subtlety for divine experience, they tried,
following the example of their master, to cultivate that
experience, and formed themselves into a society for
that purpose. This society which Jesus, with a true
comprehension of its inner character, had called the
" kingdom of heaven," or the " kingdom of God,"

---

* On the Jewish feeling with regard to God, see Prof. W.
Robertson Smith's *Prophets of Israel*, Lecture I.

was what became known later by a mere external designation as the Church. In this society the faculty of divine experience received the name of faith, which thus became the very life-principle of the new institution.

It is of the utmost importance that, before proceeding further, we should understand the nature and place of faith, and this for two reasons : (1) because it is what gives meaning and completeness to Greek education, and (2) because the failure to comprehend its sphere and its relations to reason is what has given rise to nearly all the theological and religious difficulties that have proved so detrimental to religion and to thought.

Faith, then, is the sense of the supernatural. It bears the same relation to this that the so-called bodily senses bear to the world of Nature.* And just as our reason out of bodily sensations and its own resources constructs an external physical world of related things or determined effects, so it constructs out of the data of faith and its own resources an inner moral world of related spirits or self-determining causes. Reason may err in either case, giving us a Ptolemaic astronomy or a Mohammedan religion ; but this does not affect the data of the senses, or the possibility of ultimate truth based on exhaustive experience.

It was a very long time before the Greeks discovered the relation of the faith-begotten principles of Jesus to their own intellectual and moral achievements, to the results of their own education. At

---

* " Nature is the principle of movement and change." Aristotle, *Physics*, iii, 1: 200 b 12. In this sense I am using the word.

the first glance they seemed mere foolishness.* Nor
need we wonder at this, when we consider with what
attachments of crude material myth and legend they
were first presented to them. We are certainly right
in holding that true Christianity is primitive Christianity—that is, the great life-principles proclaimed
and lived out by Jesus; but we must not forget that
these formed but a very small part of what was taught
as Christianity almost from the beginning of its career.
It took all the resources of Greek thought for centuries
to force upon what was presented as Christian truth a
meaning which intelligence could in any way accept;
and, after all, the result was one in which Jesus would
hardly have recognized anything of his own. And this
leads us to consider the relation of Christianity to Hellenism.

When Christianity appeared, it came into a world
more or less saturated with philosophic and practical
Hellenism. Not only had Greek modes of life become
generally prevalent all over the East, but Greek ways
of thinking had permeated all the religions; not, however, without being themselves, in turn, influenced
by these. The most conspicuous results of this syncretism were Neopythagoreanism, Orientalized Hellenism, Hellenized Zoroastrianism, and Hellenized Judaism, systems which were gradually replacing the elements out of which they sprang. With all of these
the supernatural teaching of Jesus came in contact

---

* This is shown in a very striking way in a *graffito* taken
from one of the prætorian guard-rooms of the palace of the
Cæsars, and now in the Kircherian Museum in Rome. It represents a Greek, Alexamenos, praying to a figure with an ass's
head nailed to a cross.

almost from the very first, and toward all of them it had to adopt a certain attitude, on pain of standing completely isolated and ineffective. To Judaism, pure and simple, it was closely related from the first, being, indeed, only the consummation of that system. Shortly after the death of its founder, when it began to make its way in the *Diaspora*, it came in contact with Hellenized Judaism, and the effect of this is already apparent in the epistles of Paul, the epistle to the Hebrews, and the gospel and epistles of John. Somewhat later, perhaps, when it began to find acceptance among the pagans, it had to encounter Neopythagoreanism and Hellenized Zoroastrianism, the former chiefly in Egypt, the latter in Syria and neighboring districts. The influence of the former is manifest in the writings of Clement of Alexandria and Origen; of the latter, in the works of the Gnostics, of Marcion, and Montanus.

Pure Judaism, in so far as it conflicted with Christianity, was practically overcome by Paul; but Hellenized Judaism proved much more formidable. "Hellenism," says Harnack, "has also a share in Paul. . . . Paul adapted the gospel of Christ to the Greek mode of thinking."* The same is true, in even a higher degree, of the author of the epistle to the Hebrews, which is deeply tinged with Aristotelianism, while the gospel and epistles of John are almost saturated with Philonism and its doctrine of the Logos. When we pass beyond the limits of the New Testament and the "apostolic" writings, we find a Christianity that has undergone the influence both of Hellenized Zoroas-

---

* *Dogmengeschichte*, vol. i, p. 83 (2d ed.).

trianism and of Orientalized Hellenism, which we may call Neopythagoreanism. In the hands of the Gnostics,* of Marcion and Montanus, it has become a dualistic theory of deliverance for man from the power of darkness, and of restoration to the kingdom of light; in those of Clement and Origen, a philosophy of ascent from the material to the ideal world. The former was combined with a theurgic, mysterious ritual; the latter with an ascetic mysticism, which finally took form in monachism. It was out of the union of all these different modifications of Christ's teaching that there resulted what is known to the world as Catholic Christianity, with its Hebrew god, its Philonian Logos, its Gnostic mysteries and ritual, and its Neopythagorean mysticism and asceticism.†

It is no part of the aim of this lecture to trace all the changes undergone by Christianity through its contact with Hellenism and Hellenized Oriental religions; my endeavor is merely to show how Hellenism was supplemented and developed through them. We have seen that, under the influence of the East, the different schools of Greek thought (excepting always the " godless Epicurean ") had taken a religious bent, and converged into what we might call Neopythagoreanism. We have likewise seen that this last deeply influenced Christianity. But the influence was not all

---

* " All are agreed that a particular person—namely, Simon the Magian, is to be regarded as the root of the heresy " (" gnosticism ").—Harnack, *Dogmengeschichte*, vol. i, p. 205 *sq.*

† Consult in this connection Drummond, *Philo Judæus;* Bigg, *The Christian Platonists of Alexandria;* Hatch, *The Influence of Greek Ideas and Usages upon the Christian Church;* Harnack, *Dogmengeschichte*, vol. i.

on one side; Christianity influenced Neopythagoreanism, and turned it into that last marvelous product of
the Greek mind, Neoplatonism.

It is usual to regard Plotinus as the founder of this
system, as he is its most distinguished exponent; but
it can hardly be said to have any founder, since it is
nothing more than the natural outcome of the tendency of Christianity to absorb Hellenism and Orientalism. In Clement and Origen the Christian element in the compound still holds the upper hand,
and, accordingly, these call themselves Christians; *
but in Ammonius Saccas, a pupil of the latter, the
balance turns the other way. He accordingly drops
the Christian name and champions a syncretism of
Gnosticism, Neopythagoreanism, and Christianity,
which later on was known as Neoplatonism. His pupil was Plotinus, of whom it has been said: "The
true Gnostic, though he repudiates the name, is Plotinus. The logical development of the thoughts of
Basilides and Justin, of Valentinus and the Naassenes,
is found in Neoplatonism—that splendid vision of incomparable and irrecoverable cloudland, in which the
sun of Greek philosophy set." † If we ask why it was
cloudland, the answer is, Because, while absorbing the
exhalations of all the great systems of thought, it re-
jected that which alone could have given them reality,
and thus, instead of disencumbering the way to heaven,

---

* Origen, however, went so far that the Alexandrine Church
expelled him, and in the fifth œcumenical council many of his
teachings were condemned. See Denzinger, *Enchiridion Sym-
bolorum et Definitionum* pp. 57–62.

† Hatch, *The Influence of Greek Ideas and Usages upon the
Christian Church*, p. 132 *sq.*

became a nebulous mass darkening the face of it. Neo-platonism, even at its best, reaches no personal, intelli-gent first principle, no being of love and choice and will, but only a bald abstraction, to which, in its desire to secure transcendence, it denies even the attribute of being. Not possessing the first condition or even the conception of concrete moral life, it can make no effort and contribute no motive, toward the realization of that life. It can only call upon men to aspire to the primal nonentity, which in no way differs from *nirvana*, by an ascetic, world-spurning process of self-emptying, which is hostile not only to the social conditions of moral life, but also to human life of any kind. Nor need we be surprised at this result. It is the only one which any system of philosophy or religion which seeks to find the Supreme Being by an intellectual process, without a supernatural experience, can possibly reach. History has demonstrated this many times. Neopla-tonism, where it is not held in subordination, is fatal to true religion, and even to true philosophy. Wherever, in its union with religion, it has gained the upper hand, it has resulted in false mysticism, morbid self-con-sciousness, paralysis of the will, moral death. The Christian Church has fought its influences for sixteen hundred years ; it is fighting them to-day. Wherever Neoplatonism gives tone to philosophy, the result is an empty dialectic idealism, arrogantly spurning the world of concrete reality.

But though Greek philosophy and Greek educa-tion, as such, came to a sad end in Neoplatonism, their career was by no means closed. They had proved, indeed, incapable by themselves of steering the ship of the world's life, and had thenceforth to take a subor-

dinate position, and sail under a flag not their own;
but under that flag, and guided by a higher hand, they
did admirable service, such as could have been performed by them alone. Of this service we shall treat
in our next chapter.

CHAPTER IX.

GREEK EDUCATION IN CONTACT WITH THE GREAT
WESTERN WORLD—RÉSUMÉ AND CONCLUSION.

I HAVE carried on the account of Hellenism in its
relations to the East until the time when it ceased to
be an independent influence. But long before that it
had entered into relations with the West, and these
were very different from the other. In the East it had
been a master; in the West it was a servant. For,
however true might be Horace's saying that "captive
Greece took captive her rude conqueror," she did not
on that account become the master of her captive, but
only his teacher, and this she could do, and did, in the
position of a slave. As a matter of fact, many very
learned Greek teachers were chattel slaves, or at best
freedmen—for example, Epictetus, Tyrannion, etc.

The Greeks seem to have come but little in contact
with the Romans until after the time of Alexander.
They are not even mentioned by any Greek author, I
think, before Aristotle. It was not till about 200 B. C.,
after the close of the second Punic war, that the Greeks
began to find their way to Rome and to exert an influence there. For some time even after that this influence was slight; but when, in the year 146, Greece became a Roman province, the Greeks began to pour into

Rome, carrying with them their culture, their education, and their philosophy. In vain did Rome try first to resist, and then to rival them. She had become a cosmopolitan state, and she had to adopt a cosmopolitan culture if she was to maintain herself as such. This culture Hellenism alone could give, and so she had to adopt Greek education and all that was implied in or followed from that—Greek art, Greek philosophy, Greek religion, Greek modes of life—in a word, Greek civilization, such as it was in the second century B. C But a borrowed civilization, like a borrowed coat, rarely fits the borrower, and so it proved in this case. What suited an intellectual, æsthetic people like the Greeks was ill adapted for an active, volitional people like the Romans. It might, indeed, polish—or rather veneer—them, but at the same time it necessarily paralyzed them. Naturally enough, too, they borrowed the husk rather than the kernel of it. The older Greek education had aimed at producing capable citizens, the later at producing sages. That which the Romans borrowed did neither. It produced mostly dilettanti and rhetoricians. Roman literature, Roman art, Roman philosophy are but feeble imitations of Greek. Whatever the Roman had to learn from the Greek, in that he was inferior to him. But there was one thing in which the Roman had nothing to learn from the Greek, and everything to teach him, and that was statesmanship, or political science. In that the Greek, at his best, was a dilettanti, while the Roman was a master, as, indeed, the actual relations of the two clearly demonstrated. Whatever, therefore, is of interest in the career of Hellenism in the West is confined to its relations with Roman statesmanship.

Rome, as a cosmopolitan state, needed—and vaguely knew that she needed—a cosmopolitan religion. Realizing that her old ethnic religion, even with Greek modifications and additions, was not equal to the need, she opened her doors freely to all religions, as if a combination of them might effect what one was unequal to; then, finding that this measure did not answer, and discovering nowhere a god who could command universal adoration, she fell upon the strange expedient of setting up her emperor as a god, building temples and altars to him, and commanding that he should be universally adored.* But though Rome could to a certain degree regulate the actions of her subjects, she could not command their wills or determine their faith. She could not turn the worship of the emperor, even though identified with her own genius, into a religion. And so the demand for a cosmopolitan religion which should supply a moral sanction for the institutions of the Roman state, as it had come to be, remained unsatisfied. Meanwhile the people lived along as best they could, either upon their old religions, or upon new religions introduced from the East, or upon some form of Greek philosophy, or, finally, without any religion at all, the resources of the state, in the form of brute force, making up to a large extent for the want of a religious or moral bond. But it was felt and recognized by all earnest and thoughtful men that this condition of things could not be permanent; that sooner

---

* Given the ideas of God prevalent at that time, this could not seem so strange or outrageous to the Romans as it does to us. See Harnack, *Dogmengeschichte*, vol. i, p. 103 *sq.* Friedländer, *Darstellungen aus der Sittengeschichte Roms*, vol. iii, p. 455 *sqq.*

or later the state must find a moral bond, if it was to exist at all, and that this moral bond must be a religion. And the demand created a supply. From time to time, ever from the establishment of the œcumenic empire, systems had risen which declared themselves capable of satisfying it. First there were the four great schools of Greek philosophy: Platonism, Aristotelianism, Stoicism, and, strangely enough, Epicureanism, each of which had a large and influential following. Then came various Eastern religions—Isisworship, Mithras-worship, etc.—which appealed to certain deep, mysterious needs of human nature, and were widely popular, all the more so that they had been greatly transformed under Greek influence. Lastly there was Judaism, compassing sea and land to make one proselyte, and making a large number in all parts of the empire. But each and all of these proved, upon trial, to lack some element necessary to insure universal acceptance. The Greek philosophies * appealed only to the few cultivated, and therefore were unfit for use as an imperial religion. The Eastern worships were too unearthly and individualistic to answer the purpose,† while Judaism was ruled out by the fact that it

---

* These had come to Rome directly from Athens soon after the conquest of Greece, and therefore unaffected by Alexandrine syncretism. Aristotelianism, having no religious leanings, never put in any claim to be a religion. It may be doubted if any one ever tried to live by it.

† If Mithras-worship could have belied its Zoroastrian dualistic origin, and done away with its burdensome, gloomy ritual, due to the same, it might have had a fair chance of becoming œcumenic. "The disciples of Mithras formed an organized church with a developed hierarchy. They possessed the ideas of mediation, atonement, and a Saviour who is human and yet

was essentially an ethnic religion, maintaining an in-
effaceable distinction between Jew and Gentile.

These were the principal systems that offered themselves when the need was first felt, and before the Alexandrine syncretisms found their way to Rome. After
that time there were three great systems which put in
claims, all of which for a certain time looked as if they
might be accepted. These, to name them in their
order, were Christianity, Neoplatonism, and Manichæism. All of them contained practically the same in-
gredients, only commingled in different proportions.
The first was prevailingly Jewish, but with a very large
admixture of Hellenism, and not a few features derived
from Zoroastrianism through Gnosticism. The second
was prevailingly Greek, but contained distinct and important elements derived from Judaism (through early
Christianity) and Zoroastrianism.* The third was fun-
damentally Zoroastrian, but contained Hellenic, Judaic,
and, it is said, even Brahmanic and Buddhistic elements.

Christianity was by two centuries first in the field.
About the year 200 A. D., when it had taken definite
form, had overcome its most insidious enemies—the
Jews and the Gnostics—and was beginning to claim
universality, it had from the simple instinct of self-
preservation become completely Hellenized. Having

---

divine, and not only the idea but the doctrine of a future life.
They had a eucharist and a baptism, and other curious analo-
gies might be pointed out between their system and the Church
of Christ.—Bigg, *The Christian Platonists of Alexandria*, p.
240.

* Plotinus made a vain effort to reach Babylon and study
Zoroastrianism at its source.—Porphyry, *Life of Plotinus*, cap. 3.

been forced to face foes clad in a panoply of Greek philosophy and rhetoric, it had in self-defense donned the same, and in doing so had transformed itself from a historical belief and a rule of life into a metaphysical theory and a creed. Looking back upon the simplicity and moral effectiveness of primitive Christianity, we may regret this as a corruption and an enfeeblement, and so, indeed, it was; but it was unavoidable, if Christianity was to outlive the direct personal influence of its founder and make its way in the great world. Moreover, in becoming Hellenized it had not laid aside the two things which distinguished it from Hellenism—its faith, or supernatural sense, and its belief in a personal God, and of a real incarnation of God in man. These were all that it had to give to Hellenism, and they were all that Hellenism lacked. For these it had fought, and was ready to fight, to the bitter end. Thus the Christianity of the third century—let us say, in a word, Catholic Christianity—was Orientalized Hellenism supplemented by faith, a supreme personal God, and an incarnate Saviour-God.

What this Hellenism amounted to without this addition we may see in Neoplatonism, which next presented itself as the universal religion. This system, as we have seen, had arisen out of a combination of Neopythagoreanism * and certain Christian tendencies derived from Origen. It seems to have been this element and earnestness that gave it consistency and force; for Neopythagoreanism without it became, after the Christian era, an ever more and more fantastic, theurgic, and

---

* Perhaps that form of it held by Numenius. See Bigg, *The Christian Platonists*, p. 250 *sqq.*

degraded system. Toward the close of the second century it tried to set itself up as a rival to Christianity, by copying its external features to mask its paganism in. For Moses it set up Pythagoras; for the Law and the Prophets, the Pythagorean, Orphic, and Platonic writings; for Jesus, Apollonius of Tyana; and for the Gospel, the romance of this man's life written by the elegant rhetorician Philostratus at the command of a Roman empress.* This foolish attempt did nothing more than show that paganism felt itself vanquished. Practical results it had none. The case was different with Neoplatonism, which, with its strong spiritual leanings and earnest desire after purity of life, discarded much that was fantastical, and sought to reach God by an ascetic intellectual process. But, in discarding the fantastical, it discarded also the supernatural sense, and in carrying its Hellenic intellectualism to its final results it reached an inane first principle, which, being beyond human knowledge, was also beyond human sympathy and love, and could therefore offer neither moral sanctions nor a basis for concrete moral life. Besides this, it labored under the difficulty which must always attach to a philosophical religion—it appealed only to the cultivated and the learned. It was, therefore, from every point of view, unfit to be a world-religion.

Almost contemporary with the rise of Neoplatonism was that of Manichæism, long supposed to have been a mere Christian heresy, but now known to have been a

---

* In reading this work one is tempted to exclaim at every page, How little did even the most cultivated Greek or Roman understand what Christianity really meant; how incapable was either of inventing it!

mixture of Zoroastrian, Chaldæan, Christian, and perhaps other elements.* Its foundation seems to have been Zoroastrian dualism. It was thoroughly materialistic and fantastical, and shows but to a very slight degree the influence of Hellenism. For this reason it lies beyond our horizon. Besides this, though it made many converts and exercised a wide influence in the East, it came too late into the West to have any chance of success.

Between these three systems, which offered to take the place of an œcumenic religion, the choice, if choice there was to be, could not be doubtful. Between (1) a religion with a personal God, incarnate in man, a high system of ethics and a principle suited to become the basis of free institutions, (2) a religion which was merely a sublimated and fanciful philosophy of nature, with neither living God nor ethical principle, and (3) a religion which was but a coarse materialism, imposing material rites, instead of moral action, as the condition of salvation, the difference was clear enough. And even had Rome hesitated to choose, it would have made no difference. Christianity conquered by its own inherent strength, which is always the best and the final test of the truth of a system. In the first quarter of the fourth century the Roman Empire, in the person of Constantine, recognized that it had found the long desiderated imperial religion, and Christianity became the religion of the state. From this time on, all other religions and all candidates for universality—pagan-

---

* On Mani and his religion, see Spiegel, *Erânische Alterthumskunde*, vol. ii, pp. 195–232; Harnack, *Dogmengeschichte*, vol. i, pp. 737–751.

ism, Neoplatonism, Manichæism—were regarded with disfavor, placed at a disadvantage, and as fast as possible proscribed.

But though Hellenized Christianity had thus triumphed, there still remained a serious difficulty. Among its professors there were wide differences of opinion as to what Christianity really was, and, while these continued, it could not truly become the religion —that is, the sustaining moral bond and sanction—of the state. Accordingly, the head of the state now set to work to bring about complete unity of opinion as to what constituted Christianity, and for this purpose called the Council of Nicæa (A. D. 325), to formulate a catholic or universal creed. In the composition of this, and the determination of its different articles, Greek philosophy played a considerable part; at the same time several definitions were made for the express purpose of checking its supremacy, and compelling it, so to speak, to accept that supplement without which it would necessarily fall back to the rank of Neoplatonism. Indeed, such would probably have been its fate had the doctrines of Arius been accepted. However repugnant, therefore, some of the articles of the Nicene Creed may be to human reason, and however true it may be that they put an end to all rational theology, it was nevertheless these very articles that saved Christianity *—and Hellenism.

---

* "One need not be an orthodox trinitarian to see that, if Arianism had had its way, the theology of Christianity would have become of a kind in which no modern philosopher, who had outgrown the demonism of ancient systems, could for a moment acquiesce."—Thomas Hill Green, *Christian Dogma*, Works, vol. iii, p. 172.

Though we may perhaps say that Neoplatonism, or pure Hellenism, was overcome at the Council of Nicæa, just as pure Judaism had been at the Council of Jerusalem, still Neoplatonism did not cease to influence Christianity, to saturate it more and more with Hellenism. Less, probably, than a hundred years after the Nicene Council, there appeared a series of works presenting a more complete syncretism between Christianity and Neoplatonism than had ever been known before. These works, long attributed—no one knows why—to Dionysius the Areopagite * (Acts, xvii, 34), profoundly influenced the teachings and practice of the Church in all succeeding ages, being the chief source of Christian mysticism and of the mediæval type of piety. Had their tendency ever completely gained the upper hand, Christianity would have become a species of Neoplatonic asceticism. Fortunately, their influence was confined to the East for many centuries.

When Hellenized Christianity became the religion of the Roman Empire it was expected to stand in the same relation of solidarity to it in which the ancient pagan religions had stood to their respective states—to form its bond and sanction. But, in reality, the attempt to make it do so was a pouring of new wine into old skins, against which Jesus had warned his followers. Christianity, whose aim was to develop the free moral personality of the individual, could not be the sanction of an institution which, with all its cosmopolitanism, had never overcome the old Greek and Roman notion that the citizen and the man are iden-

---

* See Bishop Westcott, *Religious Thought of the West*, pp. 142 *sqq.*

tical. Hence the union of church and empire could
only result in one of two things : either (1) the church
must remain a mere impotent appendage to the empire,
leaving it without any moral bond or sanction, or else
(2) it must disintegrate the empire and build up a new
institution from its own inner force. As a matter of
fact, both happened, the former in the eastern portion
of the empire, the latter in the western. In the East,
the empire fell slowly to decay for want of a combining
moral sanction ; in the West, it soon went entirely to
pieces, and on its ruins rose the Roman Catholic
Church, the true institution of Hellenized Christianity. The reason for this difference of result is due to
the fundamental difference between Greeks and Romans. The former, with their unconquerable intellectual bent, laid chief stress upon the Hellenic ideal
elements in Christianity, which were entirely incapable
of forming the bond of a concrete moral institution ;
whereas the latter, with their strong volitional and
practical tendencies, emphasized the personal and
purely Christian elements, which were admirably fitted
to be an institutional basis. The great exponent of
this Roman development is Augustine, in whom Christianity, Hellenism, and Romanism are blended in the
most fruitful way.

The Roman Catholic Church, then, is the institutional realization of Hellenism, as subrelated to, and
expository of, the teachings of Jesus, and its vigorous
life of fifteen hundred years proves the strength of the
principle which underlies it. On the other hand, the
feebleness of the Eastern Church, with its excessive
Hellenism and want of true sense of the personality
and incarnation of God, became most painfully mani-

fest when it had to encounter the strong personal
monotheism of Mohammedanism. This crude, fantastic, and material system, from which Hellenism is
absent,* but in which the supernatural sense plays a
great part, revealing the personality of God, enabled a
nation of semibarbarians to conquer the whole domain
of the Eastern Empire, and almost blot out Greek
Christianity from the face of the earth. It did the
same thing for dualistic Zoroastrianism; but, when it
tried to match itself with Western Christianity, in
which Greek idealism and Zoroastrian dualism were
held in subjection, it found a power far superior to it.
But, for all that, even Western Christianity received a
strange contribution from Islam in the shape of a fresh
accession of Hellenism.

Up to this time there was one of the great Greek
philosophies—nay, the very greatest—that had but very
slightly contributed to Christianity. This was Aristotelianism. Its turn had now come. Owing to a
series of circumstances which can not be related here,
this philosophy had come into a certain prominence in
the fifth century. Being found uncongenial to Western Christianity, and, indeed, to orthodox Christianity
generally, it had taken refuge among some heretical
Eastern sects, such as the Nestorians, whose school at
Nisibis was long an influential centre of peripateti-
cism. Thence it spread over a large portion of the
East, and was carried by physicians even into Arabia.
Hence it happened that when Islam, after the intoxi-
cation of its first triumphs, began to call for culture,

---

* It is a compound of Judaism, debased Christianity, Zoroastrianism, and possibly Manichæism.

and a rational form in which to express its victorious monotheism, it found Aristotelianism ready to its hand, and adopted it without question. Hardly anything could have been more fortunate. Owing to its combination with this all-embracing philosophy, Islam bade fair not only to conquer the world by force of arms, but also to rule it by the indefeasible right of superior intelligence. This is not the place to describe the Saracen civilization, or even its great schools in Cordova and Bagdad, to all of which the world owes so much. Suffice it to say that, through their influence, the philosophy of Aristotle became so universally popular in the twelfth and thirteenth centuries as to threaten the very foundations of the Christian religion. In course of time the Roman Church took alarm and tried to suppress the new influence; but finding this impossible, it concluded to make terms with the intruder. In consequence, the works of Aristotle, without Arab additions or interpretations, were sought out and carefully studied by the greatest intellects of the time—Alexander of Hales, Albertus Magnus, Thomas Aquinas, etc.—when it was discovered that, instead of being foes to the Church, they could be made its most effective apologists and defenders. Accordingly, in the course of a few years a new synthesis was made between Christianity and Aristotelianism, and this became thenceforth, and is to-day, the theology of the Roman Church.* The aim of this synthesis was nothing less than to reduce the whole of human knowledge to a perfect, well-rounded system culminating in the-

---

* See the present Pope's Encyclical, *Æterni Patris,* issued in 1879.

ology, whose organ was the Church and whose end the
vision of God.   In previous times, Hellenism, chiefly
of the Stoic and Platonic sort, had been employed to
give definiteness and defensible form to particular articles of faith; now, in the form of Aristotelianism, it
was used to rear an all-embracing structure, whose top,
like that of the tower of Babel, was to reach to heaven,*
and enable him who could ascend to it to enjoy the
mystic vision of God.   It is this structure that Dante
has described with such transcendent power in his
Divine Comedy, to which, as he says, "heaven and
earth put a hand."   The hands of heaven were Augustine and Dionysius; those of earth, Aristotle and
Averroës.

In reading this great work, one is tempted to believe that now, at last, Hellenism has reached its goal;
that, crowned with the concrete beliefs of Christianity,
it has elevated man to moral freedom, to the image of
God.   But it is not so; and the reasons are not difficult to discover.   They are two, and both are due
to Hellenism.   The first is, that the Church, being
organized after the model of the empire which she
had supplanted, persisted in merging the Christian in
the church-member, as the latter had merged the man
in the citizen; the second, that, following Plato, Aristotle, and Plotinus, she made the supreme end of man
consist in vision, an act of the intellect.   The former of
these defects destroyed the moral autonomy of the individual, the latter tended to withdraw him altogether
from practical life, in which the moral will finds its

---

* See Bonaventura's *De Reductione Artium ad Theologiam,*
and compare his *Itinerarium Mentis in Deum.*

chief sphere of action. The ideal of the mediæval Church is the contemplative saint ; its type of piety is mysticism,* in which not only the will, but even the intellect, is reduced to silence.† Thus the failure of the mediæval Church to satisfy the demand of the human soul for moral freedom was due to the fact that in it Hellenism, both on its practical and its speculative sides, had conquered Christianity. Practically the Church was a Platonic republic, and not a kingdom of God ; speculatively she was far more Neoplatonic than Christian, even after she had arrayed herself in Aristotelianism.‡ But with all this the Church was nourishing, in these very Hellenicisms, the germs of a reaction against herself and her claims. Mysticism is of necessity an individual matter, and tends to make the individual independent of the Church. This was

---

* " Mysticism is catholic piety generally, as far as the latter is not mere obedience to the Church—that is, implicit faith. For this reason mysticism is not one form among others of pre-Reformation piety ; . . . but it is the catholic pattern of individual piety in general."—Harnack, *Dogmengeschichte*, vol. iii, p. 375. " A mystic who does not become a catholic is a dilettante."—*Ibid.*, p. 377.

† " Do thou, O friend, proceeding boldly on the way to mystic visions, abandon the senses and the operations of the intellect ; abandon things sensible and things invisible, and all non-being and being ; and, as far as possible, unknowingly restore thyself to the unity of Him who is above all essence and all science." Quoted with approval by Bonaventura (*Itinerarium Mentis in Deum*, chap. vii), from Dionys. Areopag. (*Mystic Theol.*, chap. i, sec. 1).

‡ The mysticism of Thomas, the consummate Aristotelian, is quite as marked as that of his more Platonic contemporary Bonaventura. See Thomas à Vallgornera, O. P., *Mystica Theologia Divi Thomæ*, 2 vols., 8vo, Turin, 1890–'91.

strikingly illustrated in the German mysticism of the thirteenth and fourteenth centuries—a mysticism which not only gave birth to such associations as the Friends of God and the Brothers of Common Life (rendered forever famous by Thomas à Kempis), but also, in a degree, paved the way for Protestantism.* Aristotelian scholasticism, on the other hand, by introducing reason as a chief architect of that theology which was to be the very life-principle and sanction of the Church, opened the way for the triumph of rationalism.† The results of all this were, on the one hand, the Pagan Renaissance, which aimed at Hellenicism, pure and simple; on the other, the Protestant Reformation, which sought to extrude Hellenicism, and particularly Aristotle, from religion and the Church, and to return to pure Christianity. The former was confined to the Romance peoples, the latter to the Germanic, between whom a great gulf was thus fixed.‡

With the Pagan Renaissance and the Protestant Reformation began a new period in the progress of man toward that moral autonomy which was formulated by Socrates and translated into concrete life by Jesus. Neither of these movements in the beginning understood its own meaning, and they had little in common except an impulse toward freedom — the

---

* Luther's sympathy for the German mystics is well known.

† See Eucken, *Die Philos. des Thom. von Aquino und die Cultur der Gegenwart*, pp. 24 *sqq.*

‡ The great epopœia of this double reaction is Göthe's *Faust*, in which the nature and limitations of Hellenism are well brought out, but in which the meaning of Christianity is but poorly appreciated. Its characteristic features, indeed, are completely ignored. Göthe's sympathies were too Hellenic, Neoplatonic, and Pantheistic, to admit of any other result.

former demanding it for the sensuous and æsthetic nature, the latter for the intellect and the will. In a way they supplemented each other—a fact which Göthe observed and tried to bring out in *Faust*. Indeed, it was one of Göthe's aims to bring the two movements into fruitful connection. The effects of the new departure soon showed themselves in all departments of human activity, not only in religion but also in art, science, ethics, politics, education, and philosophy. I can not follow them into all these regions, but must content myself with taking a glance at the last two, in which we shall see clearly how completely Hellenic in its motives the whole movement was.

The education of the middle age had consisted of the "seven liberal arts," philosophy (physics, metaphysics, ethics), and theology, forming, it was thought, a natural stair from Nature up to God.* This curriculum was of Greek origin, but modified by Christian ideals, and it was a noble one, remarkable alike for its comprehensiveness, its unity, and its aimfulness. It was admirably adapted to train men for membership in the Church, and to make them loyal to its aims. It corresponded to a perfectly clear and definite view of life, its career and end, such as the Church held. With the rise of the new movement, and its twofold tendency, this definiteness was lost, and consequently education became in a measure chaotic, fragmentary, and aimless—a condition from which it has not entirely recovered even to this day.†

---

* See my *Aristotle and the Ancient Educational Ideals*, p. 239 *sqq.*

† See a forcible statement of this fact, Seeley, *Natural Religion*, p. 128.

Several of the "liberal arts" were discarded, and their place taken by the study of the Greek and Latin pagan writers. But there was no uniformity of practice, because there was no uniformity of aim. At first sight this seems very regrettable, but it could not have been otherwise. If men were to attain that autonomy which was the aim of the new epoch, they must each set his own aim and select that education which seemed most likely to lead him to it. It necessarily took—let us rather say, it necessarily will take—a long time for men exercising moral freedom to recognize that that freedom can never become actual and concrete until they all have a common aim, and work freely and unitedly toward that. Until then education will not attain the unity, comprehensiveness, and aimfulness which it had in the middle age.

The same change that took place in education took place in philosophy. Mediæval philosophy had had a perfectly definite aim, which was, to act as a handmaid to theology, and show that the facts of the world and of life were in perfect harmony with revealed truth. *Credo ut intelligam :* first faith, and then philosophy to justify it. Under the new movement all was different. The Pagan Renaissance did not profess to know where philosophy might lead, and so contented itself for the most part with studying Plato and Plotinus and questioning Nature, thus laying the foundations of modern science. The Protestant Reformation, on the other hand, with a correct instinct, distrusted philosophy as a means of reaching divine truth, and therefore devoted little attention to it. After a time, however, individuals more or less impregnated with the Protestant spirit engaged in free speculation, and naturally came to very diverse results. Some, like the Oxford Platonists, turned back to the ancient thinkers; but the majority trusted to their own unaided intelligence. If Protestantism looked askance at Philosophy, Philosophy responded by going its own way independently of Protestantism. In one respect this was a great advantage, in that Philosophy was thus able to unfold itself independently of authority; in another, it was a great disadvantage, in that it fell out of relation to theology, and altogether ignored that sphere of experience from which religion draws its life. It thus remained, and remains, essentially at the Hellenic stage. Of the two most fruitful philosophies that arose under Protestant influence, that of Descartes and that of Locke, the former, in the hands of Wolf, ended in pure metaphysical formalism; the latter, in those of Hume, in absolute skepticism; and when Kant attempted to construct a philosophy by uniting the two, he only paved the way for Hegelianism and Schopenhauerianism, the former of which is only a modernized form of Neoplatonic Gnosticism, while the latter is little more than Orientalized Stoicism. Both may now be said to be obsolete, and the Protestant world to be without a philosophy. The same cause which led to the decay of ancient philosophy has brought about that of modern philosophy— the neglect of the supernatural sense. Ignore this, and philosophy necessarily ends in either pure formalism, pure skepticism, pure mysticism, or pure pessimism.

Comparing the colossal results attained by mediæval thought with the meagre and uncertain products of modern speculation, we can hardly help feeling as the Israelites did when in the barren wilderness they sighed for the fleshpots of Egypt. But it may be well to bear in mind that they were on the way to the promised land, and that their meagre fare, which could not be kept overnight, was after all from heaven. The promised land of humanity is moral freedom, which implies individual insight and conviction, and those who are striving after these and refusing to accept any truth on external authority are on the way thither, no matter what sandy tracks, monsters, and hobgoblins they may have to encamp among overnight. The truth is, the chaotic condition in which all the departments of human life are at this moment need cause us neither regret nor apprehension. It is simply the first result of man's attempt to live a free moral life, to direct his steps in accordance with the universal element in him; and the more fearlessly he persists in this attempt, the more will the harmonizing and unifying power of that element become manifest and actual, the more will universal freedom be realized.

In our endeavors toward this we shall be aided in avoiding rocks and pitfalls by a careful study of the career of Greek education and culture, whose history, on the whole, has been the history of human freedom. Let us take, as it were, a bird's-eye view of it, marking its chief stages.

Greek education and culture began with the natural family or tribe, which, like every institution of culture, was held together by a religious bond. In this instance the bond was one of blood, whose corresponding ritual was a meal or feast, at which a member of the tribe, an animal or a man, was slain and its flesh partaken of by all the other members, a portion being set apart for the dead members, whose shades were the only gods. This was the stage of animism. In course of time, as the family merged in the phratry, the blood-bond was supplemented by the land-bond, the ancestor-gods by Nature-gods, and the sacrifice by the offering. This is the stage of natural polytheism. Later still, when the phratry was subordinated to the city-state, the older bonds were supplemented by a worth-bond (ἀρετή), and a line was drawn between gentle and simple. The Nature-deities were now superseded by moral deities, and prayer was added to sacrifice and offering. This is the stage of moral polytheism, gradually tending toward monotheism, which, however, it never reached among the Greeks as a people.

It was only at this stage that a distinction began to be felt between the natural and the supernatural. Previously the supernatural had been included in the natural. All things were full of gods, as Thales said. But now the distinction obtruded itself, and with it the distinction between the natural senses and the supernatural sense, and henceforth the course of education was determined by the latter. It was only now, indeed, that conscious, systematic education, such as called schools into existence, could begin. For a time the Greek thinkers made an effort to bring the object of the supernatural sense into consciousness and to make it the rule of life. This is evident in the writings of Pherecydes and the other theologians (θεολόγοι), and of Æschylus. But after a time attention concentrated itself upon the natural, and gave birth to philosophy instead of to theology. The results of this were strange and far-reaching. Setting out with nature alone, and working by purely abstract processes up from

it, the Greeks finally arrived at a supreme principle
which was merely the last abstraction of reason. This
idol, called by various names—Reason, Being, Intellect,
etc.—they elevated into the place of God, and from it
they were never afterward able to free themselves.
Their God, instead of being the concrete object of
the supernatural sense, remained an abstraction from
nature to the very last. This is the weakness of Hellenism, and the reason why it never overcame polytheism. Socrates, indeed, in whom the supernatural sense
was strong, made an effort in the other direction, and
showed in his life and in his death the moral value of
that sense; but he never reached clearness with regard
to the supernatural, and he had no successors. Plato
and Aristotle both returned to the abstract God of
Nature, and thus determined the whole subsequent
course of Greek thought. When the nation rose po-
litically above the city-state, and needed a divinity to
be the soul and sanction of an œcumenic empire, the
Greek consciousness had none to offer—nothing but a
pale, lifeless abstraction. Even the ideal city-states of
Plato and Aristotle proved utterly incapable of realization, and after a time the whole of Greece became a
subject province of a foreign empire, thus paying
dearly for her neglect of the supernatural. Doubtless
her philosophy would have sunk into oblivion before
the religious spirit, had it not allied itself with systems of thought that were founded upon the supernatural sense. Among these the highest and purest
was that of the Jews, whose culmination was the
teaching of Jesus. Allying itself with pre-Chris-
tian Judaism, it produced Philonism; crowning
itself with the gospel of Jesus, it gave Catholic

Christianity, which finally became the religion of the œcumenic empire.

This gospel-crowned Hellenism might have been the power which was to raise mankind to that moral autonomy which Socrates had promised and Jesus exemplified, had it been content to wear its crown in meekness. Instead of this, however, it continually tried to rend it, or cast it aside, and to substitute for it the Bacchic wreath of abstract naturalism. Wearing this, it could only offer external discipline for inward freedom, mysticism for piety, and asceticism for moral life. Even when, with the aid of Aristotle, it succeeded in calling into existence an institution animated by its own spirit, it only prepared the way for its own repudiation by the spirit of freedom. This, by raising up the Pagan Renaissance and the Protestant Reformation, started a new movement, in which the world is now engaged, and which, if the lessons of past history be only heeded, may at last conduct humanity to the promised land of moral freedom. And these lessons are not difficult to enumerate. The first is, that reason, abstracting from nature, can never, apart from the object of the supernatural sense, reach a first principle that will give effective sanction to moral life, or form the basis of a free social institution, but only a moral despotism, expressing itself in mysticism and asceticism. The second is, that, until the supernatural sense can recognize in its object a living God, or Being of perfect intelligence, love, and will, supernally correlated, but in no sense identical, with the spirits of men, so that His perfections are their goal, and not His being their grave, it will never be fully able to maintain its throne against the claims of the

16

abstracting reason,* or supply the basis of moral life. This was strikingly illustrated in the case of Kant, whose supernatural sense, which he termed, strangely enough, the "practical reason," yielded him only a "categorical imperative," the conditions of which— God, freedom, immortality—his "pure reason" could only postulate, but never know as really existing. Such an imperative—a law without lawgiver, meaning, or sanction—could of course have neither moral nor organizing power. The third lesson is, that, while the hypostases reached through the supernatural sense must be carefully connected and correlated with the abstract laws reached through the natural senses, the two orders of results must be held strictly distinct. Infinite harm has come from neglecting this lesson. On the one hand, science, which is the system of laws abstracted from the data of the natural senses, has been called upon to demonstrate the existence of God and the authority of the moral law ; on the other, theology, which is the system of the hypostases reached

---

* Although it is reason that interprets the data of the supernatural sense, as well as those of the natural senses, it acts differently in the two cases. In dealing with the latter, it abstracts and generalizes; in dealing with the former, it concretes and individualizes—in a word, hypostasizes—and the one process is as legitimate as the other. One defect of Hellenism was that it failed to recognize the nature and legitimacy of the latter process. It was, indeed, ready enough to turn an adjective—good, intelligent, or the like—into a noun; but such a noun is not a hypostasis. The same is true of Hegelianism, which tries to find a supreme principle not in one abstraction of the reason, as Hellenism did, but in the organized sum of all of them. It was therefore perfectly consistent in placing philosophy above religion, as all true Greek thought had done before it.

through the supernatural sense, has been looked to for
an explanation of the natural world. Laplace has been
blamed for not employing the " hypothesis " of God in
his *Mécanique Céleste*, and Jesus for not expounding
the Copernican theory of astronomy.* In this way
science and religion have both been discredited, and
enmity has been stirred up between them, so that science has often become faithless, and religion ignorant
and prejudiced. The future of both depends largely
upon the removal of this enmity.

Finally, the fourth lesson of history is, that, of all
the faculties of the human soul, that which demands
the most careful training is the supernatural sense.

---

* " The fundamental prejudice of scholasticism—shared, indeed, by ancient and, alas! by modern theology—was, that theology is natural science (*Welterkennen*), or at least is bound to
ground and complete such science. At the present day, when
we say that it is bound to help out, to step in where science fails,
we are trying, with forced modesty, to say the same thing."—
Harnack, *Dogmengeschichte*, vol. iii, p. 313, note. " The true
relation (of the Church to science) does not consist in her always
adopting the most recent theories, but in rendering herself independent of scientific and philosophic theories altogether. 'What
I offer,' she must say, 'remains true, whether Copernicus or Ptol-
emy, whether Darwin or Agassiz, is right. The gospel neither
is, nor has, any system of cosmology or biology: it is the announcement of the kingdom of God, which is seeking to realize
itself in the hearts (*Gemüth*) and lives of men. It does not seek
support in inexplicable natural occurrences and miracles, but
upon experiences of the heart, which finds peace and blessedness
in it.'"—Paulsen, *Einleitung in die Philosophie* (1892), p. 165.
I quote these passages to show that the true relation between
the natural and supernatural is becoming clear to modern
thinkers. The second, however, is from a work which is a
warning example of what an earnest thinker may come to who

While it remains undeveloped all other education leads
ultimately to nothing.   It was the failure to recognize
this that made Greek education impotent to save the
world, and forced it to crown itself with Christianity,
whose function it is to train the supernatural sense to a
recognition of the living God as the Father of Spirits,
the sanction of the moral law, and the bond of institutional life.

If, now, reverting to our first chapter and the outline of a complete education there attempted, we compare Greek education in its system and results with
that outline, we shall be able to form some estimate of
its merits and defects. The first, it will be seen, are
very numerous.   Greek education did at every period
of its career seek with all the means in its power, by a
graded process of rational discipline, to lift men out of
the bonds of animal necessity into moral freedom as
the Greeks conceived it.   It was at all times marked
by unity, comprehensiveness, and aimfulness.   It left
no part of man's nature, known as such, uncared for.
And so successful was it, so much did it transmute
and elevate human nature, that to the Greeks is justly
accorded the honor of having discovered the principle
of human freedom, and of having placed the sword of
victory in the hands of Reason.   They not only lifted
the world out of barbarism, but it requires their influence even to this day to prevent it from falling back
into the same.   Even Christianity itself has sunk into

---

does not know the nature of the supernatural faculty, but con-
founds it (as Tennyson does, see *In Memoriam*, cxxiv, 4) with
the heart. Paulsen arrives at pure pantheism, and Tennyson
came perilously near the same. Of modern thinkers, Spicker
(see p. 138) comes nearest the truth.

barbarism and superstition wherever it has withdrawn itself from Greek influence.* So much for the merits of Greek education. Its defects are all summed up in one. By substituting philosophy for religion; by cultivating unduly the abstract reason, which is the organ of the former, and ignoring the supernatural sense, which is the condition of the latter; by placing the supreme activity of man in intellectual vision, instead of in moral life guided by vision, love, and a good will, it failed to put itself in living relation to the supreme principle of that moral freedom which is the " chief end of man." In consequence, Greece not only perished herself, but she left an example by following which other nations have perished—yea, and other nations will yet perish, unless, warned by her fate, they make all education culminate in the culture of the spiritual sense which reveals God, and so place religion on the throne that belongs to her as the guide and inspiration of life. Thus, as Christianity without Hellenism sinks into barbarism, so Hellenism without Christianity leads to destruction. Only when united, as humanity and divinity, do they lead to life and freedom.

---

* Speaking of the decay of the Eastern churches that separated from Catholicism, D. K. Müller says, " This result may enable us to estimate what the fact of the Hellenization of Christianity during the first centuries meant—its rescue from barbarism."—*Kirchengeschichte*, vol. i, p. 281.

(13)

THE END.